The Power Of Praise

by

GWEN R. SHAW

Engeltal Press
P. O. Box 447
Jasper, ARK 72641-0447
www.engeltalpress.com

Copyright 2000 by Gwen R. Shaw
End-Time Handmaidens, Inc.

Printed in the United States of America

INDEX

Foreward IV

Chapter 1 The Missionary Barrel 1

Chapter 2 Praise Has the Power to Create 7

Chapter 3 Praise Will Usher You Into the Glory of God 12

Chapter 4 Praise Will Make Provision for All Our Needs 21

Chapter 5 Praise Opens the Closed Doors 29

Chapter 6 Praise Brings Revival 34

Chapter 7 When Our Prayers are Accompanied with Praise We can come Immediately Into God's Presence 38

Chapter 8 The Sacrifice of Praise 44

Chapter 9 Praise Defeats Demonic Powers, and Drives Away Demons 53

Chapter 10 The Importance of Musical Instruments in Praise 59

Chapter 11 Hebrew Words for Praise 68

Chapter 12 Exchange Your Spirit of Heaviness For the Garment of Praise 73

FOREWARD

Spirit-filled people are "praisers" because they are full of the Holy Spirit who is the original "praiser." He is the One who taught us how, and inspires us to praise the Lord!

Praise is the expression of Heaven. And when we praise the Lord we receive Heavenly rays of light, and release the same vibrations to the world.

Praisers are conductors of power who allow the "electricity" of God's power to flow through them.

Praisers live in two places at the same time: their bodies are dwelling on earth while their spirits are in the Throne-Room Presence of the Almighty. That is what makes them so different from the rest of the human race. They are an awesome generation.

Because of their uniqueness they are so different that they are sometimes misunderstood, because it is hard to dwell in the High and Lofty Place, and still communicate with others in a normal way.

Praisers get homesick for Heaven. They long for the Glory.

All of us who expect to go to Heaven need to understand what Heaven will be like. It will be one eternal "Praise-meeting."

So, if you want to enjoy eternity, start praising God today, and you will build yourself a "runway" from which you will one day "take-off" for the wonders that await us all in Beulah Land.

I trust you enjoy this little Bible-study on praise. And that it will help you to be a better "Praiser."

Gwen R. Shaw

CHAPTER ONE

THE MISSIONARY-BARREL

I will never forget the missionary story I read many years ago about the "faith missionary" who was living in China. She had gone to China by faith, trusting in the Lord alone to meet all her needs. But there were times when it seemed that the "barrel of meal" was about to waste, and the "cruse of oil" to fail (1 Kings 17:16), because God's people were not faithful to send their support to her when the Holy Spirit spoke to them.

One month she was having an especially difficult time. Her faith was being greatly tested because the supplies had run very low. Her "missionary barrel" where she kept her supplies was almost empty. When she looked into it her heart nearly failed.

She knew that God has promised in His Word that He would supply all her needs according to His riches in Glory by Christ Jesus (Philippians 4:19), but it seemed to be only an empty promise.

Then the Lord told her that she must do an act of faith. He told her to shout into the empty barrel the praises of God. It seemed a foolish thing to do, but she had nothing to lose, so she began to praise the Lord and shout His praises into the empty barrel. She did this for several days. At first, nothing happened, then, all of a sudden, the windows of Heaven were opened and the Lord began to meet her needs. It wasn't long before the barrel was again filled with supplies.

Many times, during the years that I have served the Lord as a missionary in China, I too have claimed Philippians 4:19 and "shouted the praises of God into empty barrels" and seen the Almighty Jehovah-Jireh meet my desperate needs. Never, in the twenty-three years that I served Him among the Chinese people, living the faith-life, in China, Taiwan and Hong Kong have I ever known God to fail to meet my needs, or the needs of my family. He always supplied: the rent, the food, the clothing for my three sons, their father and me, our amah, a car, furniture, travel, whatever —. Today I trust Him to meet the daily needs of our entire missionary ministry of The End-Time Handmaidens and Servants. And though the needs are much greater than they were when I was young in faith, the supply is also greater because our faith has grown to meet the demand, as we praise the Lord daily for all His goodness.

It is easy to become fearful when we have a special need. We fear that we may "starve to death", or we fear that our children will become sick from being undernourished. Satan torments us with these kinds of fears.

But when we praise the Lord we banish the spirits of fear and distrust. Faith rushes in to take the place of fear. And with faith comes hope and trust. That is when God is able to move on our behalf. Praise is a multiplier. And praise comes from a thankful heart.

THE MIRACLE OF MULTIPLICATION

One of the usually forgotten aspects of the multiplication of the loaves and fishes is the part about the basket. The disciples brought Jesus the five loaves and two fishes. He first blessed and thanked God for what

He had. While thanking the Father, the miracle of multiplication was released from the Throne of God. As He broke the bread and fish into pieces they kept multiplying until there were so many that there was enough for each disciple to carry a basket of them to the hungry people. When they were finished feeding the five thousand men (there were also thousands of women and children) the twelve baskets were still full.

All that is wonderful, but one of the most wonderful parts of the story is that, not only were the bread and fish multiplied, the baskets were also multiplied. Otherwise, where would twelve large baskets come from? Our Jehovah-Jireh can not only send the food for our cupboards, He can supply big enough cupboards and pantries to store it in until we have need of it. Remember, Joseph's faith in the seven year abundant miracle supply inspired him to be ready to store each year's bounteous harvest. Are you prepared for all God wants to give you and do in your life? God is bigger than Joseph! Praise Him until the supply, and more comes in.

PRAISE DESTROYS THE POWER OF FEAR

Praise is very powerful. It has the power to destroy fear. Fear will paralyze you and keep you from obeying the will of God. It will hinder you from being your best for God. It will rob you of your eternal destiny. Fear blinds you. It keeps you from seeing the greatness of God. Many of God's children never climb their mountain or finish their race because they are hindered through fear. Fear causes unbelief. Unbelief is a sin because it doubts God's goodness and greatness. Fear is sin. It grieves the Lord. It puts a wall between us and God, thereby making Him feel far away.

But when you begin to praise the Lord a miracle happens, for fear is cancelled out through the power of praise. If you will begin to praise God, even when you do not feel like it, you will be set free of fear, and you will be able to see how Great God is, and this will enable you to conquer your doubts which grieve the Lord and keep Him from being able to do that miracle which you are in such great need of right now.

Don't ignore your problem, hoping it will go away. If the missionary had said to herself, "I will not accept that empty barrel. I will believe that it is full," she would not have been facing reality. She would have been in delusion. Instead, she faced the facts and praised God for what He was going to do for her. Honesty makes us face the facts and praise the Lord for the miracle that will change the situation.

We hold in our hands the keys to a miracle, but we do not use them because we don't know the power of praise.

NEVER ALLOW YOUR CIRCUMSTANCES TO ROB YOU OF YOUR JOY

We are a generation that has been spoiled by our abundance. We get what we want and we want more than our wants. In fact, we never seem to stop wanting more. There is always one thing more that we want.

This leads to discontentment. And the discontented person finds it hard to praise the Lord.

We have been brainwashed into thinking that "things" can make us happy, that wealth is the key to joy, that being loved satisfies the heart, that troubles are an indication that God is against us.

We need to wake up and realize that our joy is not determined by the things we possess. Joy is a Person, and His name is Jesus. On the night He was crucified, He was handing out the gift of joy to His disciples. And we too, because He lives in us, have the ability to give joy to others under the most difficult circumstances.

Don't only give others joy, give Jesus joy. Seek ways to make Him happy. Little acts of kindness, little deeds of sacrifice, a smile that is directed "God-ward" or a whisper, "I love You" can give Jesus so much happiness. Do the same with your Father in Heaven. Tell the Holy Spirit how much you appreciate His help and Companionship. And never neglect to "entertain angels."

When you Praise the Lord you give Him great joy because there are so many who blaspheme His name. Lucifer was thrown out of Heaven because of blasphemy against God. Many will be thrown out of the presence of God because of the same great sin, but Praise helps to give balance and light and mercy from the heart of God for this evil generation for a little while longer.

God needs "praisers" in every country, state, province, county, city, village, hamlet and home. He needs them in the workplace, He needs them in the schools, the hospitals, the mines, every airplane that flies, every train and bus that moves, every department store, every church, everywhere. God needs praisers. Without them, we will all be destroyed.

PRAISE YE THE LORD!

STUDY QUESTIONS

1. Read Matthew 14:13-21, Mark 6:30-44; Luke 9:10-17; John 6:1-4 and compare the story with Matthew 15:32-39 and Mark 8:1-10.

2. Memorize Philippians 4:19 *"But my God shall supply all your need according to his riches in glory by Christ Jesus."*

3. What does praise destroy?

4. What can help to save the world in this evil day? Why?

5. Why do "faith-missionaries" need to know how to praise the Lord?

CHAPTER TWO

PRAISE HAS THE POWER TO CREATE

When the Lord God created the heavens and earth He was surrounded by praises.

In the thirty-eighth chapter of Job God is revealing some of the secrets of creation. He asks Job, *"Where wast thou when I laid the foundations of the earth? Declare, if thou hast understanding. Who hath laid the measures thereof, if thou knowest, or who laid the corner stone thereof; When the morning stars sang together, and all the sons of God shouted for joy?"* (Job 38:4-7).

Miracles happen when holy people praise a Holy God! It is not enough just to hope and wish that a certain thing will happen. We are co-workers with God. We are Kingdom people who will rule and reign with Him over this earth when His Kingdom comes.

This we all believe; but we must also understand that Jesus said that the Kingdom of God is within us NOW. So we should take hold of this truth and use our God-given authority.

God is waiting for us to recognize our authority, which He has given to us. God is looking for someone who will act in faith so that He can move. When we begin to praise the Lord we make it possible for God to respond to our faith. We are co-regents with Him. He wants to honour us by doing miracles which can be identified with our acts of faith. Someone has said, "God makes prayer from our side the condition for His working."

If prayer can move the hand of God, think how much more praise can move Him. Prayers can be uttered mingled with unbelief, but when we begin to praise, we banish unbelief, thereby making our "praise-prayers" that much more powerful.

PRAISE GOD BEFORE YOU GET THE ANSWER

It doesn't take great faith to praise God after you have the answer to your prayers. The test of true faith is praising BEFORE you even have any sign of your prayers being answered, your need being met, or your body is healed.

The devil will tell you that you are a fool when you start to praise God for a miracle, even though it seems impossible. But never mind! Even though God may not grant us the desire we are seeking from Him, the day will come we will know and understand why we received His Best, even though it was not what we desired. God never makes a mistake. And we will be rewarded for praising the Lord even though His answer was the opposite of what we desired.

In the Great Faith Chapter of Hebrews Eleven we read about the men and women of God whose faith put them in the Hall of Fame. But in closing, the writer mentions some unnamed saints who are also great even though they did not see their prayers answered. Meditate on these words, *"And others had trial of cruel mockings and scourgings, yea, moreover of bonds and imprisonment: They were stoned, they were sawn asunder, were tempted, were slain with the sword: they wandered about in sheepskins and goatskins; being destitute, afflicted, tormented; (Of whom the world was not worthy:) they wandered in deserts, and in mountains, and in dens and caves of the earth. And these all, having obtained a good report through faith, received not the promise: God having provided some better thing for us, that they without us should not be made perfect"* (Hebrews 11:36-40).

These all obtained a good report through faith, even though they did not receive the promise. You may not get your promise, but you will still be rewarded for your faith.

The reason they did not receive the answer to their prayers was because God was using them to be an example to us that if they could still love God and be faithful to Him in spite of all their great trials, we can also go through these same fiery trials and not lose our faith in God.

That tells me that the child of God who was told that he or she would die of cancer, refused all medical treatment, and was hanging on to God for a miracle, but died in the end, will receive as great a reward in Heaven as the one who experienced a miracle of healing.

We judge by the outward appearances, but God judges by what is taking place in the heart.

Job was an example of perfect faith in God when he said, *"Though He slay me, yet will I trust Him"* (Job 13:15).

WERE WE SINGING WITH THE "CREATION CHOIR?"

Looking back at Job 38:7,8 we see that while God was creating the heavens and earth and all the things in it the mighty choirs of Heaven were singing and rejoicing. Praises filled the infinity of space as the sun, moon and stars were created, the mountains, hills and valleys took shape, the rivers, lakes and seas bubbled with crystal clear water, the trees, grasses and flowers blossomed in splendid colours, the waters filled with sparkling fishes of all sizes, the skies with creatures as small as butterflies and large as eagles, and animals came into existence. But when God created Adam, what a Hallelujah Chorus must that have inspired! And when Eve was taken out of Adam and then wedded to him in holy wedlock what anthems of love and praise must have filled the skies!

LET US FILL OUR HOMES AND LIVES WITH PRAISE

Husbands and wives need to have more music in their homes. We need songs of love and praise — love for each other and for God, praises to God for each other and for God. We need more gratitude, for praise is the expression of gratitude. It is because we have so little gratitude that the world is falling apart. We take each other for granted. We even take God for granted. "Thank You" has become a term of politeness, and not of genuine appreciation.

And then, how often do we remember to say, "Thank you!"

If praise has the power to create, why don't we praise God more? We can create things into existence through our praises alone. Praise moves the heart of God and makes my will His own.

If we do not use this power to move Heaven, when it is available to us, we are foolish. In fact, the entire Church is missing one of the great keys of authority. We sing one hymn of praise on Sunday morning and then we wonder why we are so weak spiritually, physically and morally. We need to bring praise back into the House of God!

STUDY QUESTIONS

1. Read Genesis chapter one and Job 38 and 39.

2. Memorize Job 13:15.

3. How do we know that praising God has creative power?

4. Will the person who dies of cancer, while still hoping for his healing till the last breath receive as great a reward in Heaven as the one who is miraculously healed and lives a longer life?

5. How can we make our homes a happier place to live in?

CHAPTER THREE

PRAISE WILL USHER YOU INTO THE GLORY OF GOD

When I was first saved I was taught the necessity of being filled with the Holy Spirit. At first I did not want to be like those strange "Pentecostals" who spoke in tongues and acted abnormal in their zeal for God. I wanted to be a good Christian without all that "fanaticism."

But the Holy Spirit "played a trick on me!" I went to the Pentecostal church in our city to hear two women preachers. Their dedication and their message touched my heart. When the invitation was given for everyone to go to the prayer room to pray I got up and followed the crowd. I had been saved one month.

During those days I was going through a time of testing in my young Christian walk. I had been told that, as a Christian, I would have to lay my unsaved fiancee on the altar. We had been close since childhood, and had planned eventually to marry. So this was not an easy thing for me to do. I was having a big struggle.

That Sunday night, after hearing Miss Parmenter give her testimony of being raised from the dead, and Miss Allen, her co-worker, I was in need of a touch from God, for I was wavering in my dedication to the Lord.

As I knelt down in the prayer room and began to pray, I soon was lost in God. The Presence of the Holy Spirit came down on me and all around me. I can't remember anyone praying for me or with me, but I certainly felt an unspeakable power of God resting upon me. My spirit was lifted up above my circumstances; all pain, all hurt, all grief disappeared as the Lord, Himself came very close to me. I found myself praising Him and worshipping Him as I never had done before. All I could do was cry out to Him, "Glory, glory, glory!" Truly His glory was all over me and I was lost in Him. I was literally "lost in God, shut in with Him in the secret place. There in His Presence, beholding His face."

When the Spirit began to lift, I opened my eyes and found that so much time had passed that almost everyone had left except for one sister. She had stayed to pray with me.

I dried my eyes and smiled. I felt so good, so clean, so holy. She said to me, "Gwenny, you almost received the Baptism of the Holy Spirit!"

I was shocked. I didn't want this so called "Baptism of the Holy Spirit" that made these Pentecostals do such peculiar things.

I asked her, "Is that what the Baptism of the Holy Spirit is like?"

She answered, "Yes, only more-so! More glory, more blessing, more power, more of Jesus!"

All this had come upon me because I had praised Him. It was so easy. No works, no great sacrifices, no special virtues or good deeds — just praise!

I knew that what I had experienced was real. I could never, in all my life have manufactured or imagined the glory that I had experienced. I was convinced that what these people had was real, and I wanted it!

Three days later, in my bedroom, during a time of prayer, the spirit of praise fell upon me and I was swept up into the glorious Presence of God, and mightily filled with His Holy Spirit. My life has never been the same since then. His glory has accompanied me from then on. And it is not only around me, it is in me.

And it all began when I started praising Him in spite of my broken heart.

PRAISE WILL HEAL THE BROKEN IN HEART

There are few more miserable and unhappy women in the world than the women who have to share their husbands with a second or third wife. I know, because I lived in the Orient where some of my friends were wife number one, number two or number three. Some Chinese men had even more wives. The Moslem men are supposed to be limited to having only four wives, but often they divorce one so that they can marry another.

Sometimes these women fight and hate each other. At times they are able to live in separate houses, but most of the time they are under the same roof. They suffer terribly from jealousy, and compete with each other for their husband's affections, and if not that, at least honour. One of the ways they can get honour is through the sons they bear for their husband. They try to have a child every year. Since this is now forbidden in China, and having more than one wife is frowned upon by the Chinese Communist government, things have changed a great deal in recent years. But I lived in China when the customs were different.

Polygamy is as old as the Bible. The first man to take two wives was Lamech, a descendent of Cain, the murderer of his brother (Genesis 4:19-24). He seems to have been a violent man because he killed someone and vindicates himself by saying that he was paying him back for what the man had done to him.

Before long, the practice of taking more than one wife (which was God's original plan) was adopted by the pre-flood inhabitants of the earth. It became so bad that the Bible says, *"The sons of God saw the daughters of men that they were fair; and they took them wives of all which they chose"* (Genesis 6:2). The population of the earth began to multiply with these polygamous marriages, and sin and corruption increased greatly, until God became vexed with the evil and sent the Great Flood which destroyed a generation of humanity, saving only Noah and his family.

But as men began to multiply again after The Flood, polygamous marriages were the custom. Even good men had two wives, Abraham had two, and both of his grandsons, Esau and Jacob had more than one wife.

It was the first wife of Jacob, Leah, who suffered greatly because she was not loved by her husband. He preferred her sister Rachel who had been the passion of his life, and for whom he had worked for seven years.

PRAISE WILL HEAL THE SICK IN BODY

Praising the Lord releases rays of healing from the wounds of Jesus. A dear friend of ours, Dr. Richard Ebby, told us of his miraculous healing from a "near death" experience, in which he believes he died and went to Heaven, but was restored to life miraculously. He had fallen from a second story veranda, landed with his head on the pavement below, cracked open his skull and was pronounced dead by the medical team who came in the ambulance to take him to the emergency ward. After his miraculous healing, he still often suffered severe pains from his injuries. He told us that as long as he praised the Lord every day he retained his strength to carry on as a medical doctor for many years.

He thought he would put "praising the Lord" to the test. So one Monday he did not praise the Lord. The next day he felt uncomfortable. He did not praise the Lord that day, either. Wednesday he was in much pain. Thursday he was silent, and he was so sick, he could hardly get out of bed. By Friday he felt he was dying. So he quickly decided to praise the Lord, and immediately he began to feel better. He is still living today, and praising the Lord.

PRAISING THE LORD
MAKES MIRACLES HAPPEN

One of our End-Time Handmaidens on our staff, Valerie Devlin shares this story with us: "A number of years ago we had weekly meetings on Friday night. We would praise, worship, pray, intercede and travail. One week, the power of God fell in such a powerful way during the praise and worship, that it was 2 A.M. before we realized how late it was — certainly too late to pray for all the requests we had voiced before the meeting. Some felt sad, as the requests were very pressing.

But the Word of the Lord came forth, and He told us He had heard all the prayers that were on our hearts that day — both those we had shared, and those that were hidden in our hearts, and He would answer us.

The next two weeks we had a number of calls reporting how answers had come forth as a result of our praise and worship and dancing that night. We had one healing of cancer, one healing of heart disease, captives were set free, souls were saved, and many more wonderful things happened — all because we had praised the Lord.

LEAH WON HER HUSBAND'S LOVE THROUGH PRAISE

God saw that Leah was rejected; He heard her weeping through the night, and counted her tears. Then He acted. He opened her womb to bear children, and He closed Rachel's.

The Bible says, *"Leah conceived, and bore a son, and she called his name Reuben: for she said, Surely the Lord hath looked upon my affliction; now therefore my husband will love me"* (Genesis 29:32).

But he didn't!

A second time she conceived, and gave birth to a son. She still had hope to win Jacob's love and she said, *"Because the Lord hath heard that I was hated He hath therefore given me this son also: and she called his name Simeon"* (Genesis 29:33).

Still Jacob did not love her.

But Leah kept trying. She conceived the third time, and gave birth to a son, and said, *"Now this time will my husband be joined to me, because I have born him three sons: therefore was his name called Levi"* (Genesis 29:34).

Her three sons gave her great honour among her family and neighbours, but it did not make the heart of her husband love her.

Then Leah conceived again. When her fourth son was born she said, *"Now will I praise the Lord:"* She called him Judah" (Genesis 29:35).

The names of Leah's four sons all meant something. They revealed the struggle she was having in her heart.

Reuben: means "Behold, a son." She was trying to get Jacob's attention to the fact that she had born him a son.

Simeon: means "to hear." The great prayer of Israel, prayed in every synagogue begins with the words, "Shema Israel..." (Hear, O Israel...). The name expressed her heart's cry to God for Him to hear her prayers for her husband's love, and it was also a statement that God heard her when she prayed.

Levi: means "to be joined." It was a declaration of hope and faith.

But Judah was the ultimate key to victory, for it means "praise." It was only after Leah began to praise the Lord, in spite of circumstances, that she was able to break free from the yoke of grief, and the terrible struggle for recognition and acceptance that had tormented her. From then on, every time she called his name she was praising the Lord.

When we begin to praise the Lord our circumstances will take a turn for the better. Praise moves the hand of God and enables Him to act on our behalf. It has creative power.

Although Leah did not immediately see any dramatic change, things had been set in motion and nothing would ever be the same any more. For God saw fit to take Rachel to Himself in childbirth, and she was buried at Bethlehem. Leah spent the rest of her life as Jacob's wife and companion. When she died, she was laid to rest in the ancestral tomb in Hebron where Isaac and Rebekah, Abraham and Sarah were resting. And Jacob's dying request was that his body should be carried back to Canaan and laid to rest beside his beloved Leah (Genesis 49:29-33).

That, my friend, is the power of praise. Woman! If you would stop nagging and complaining to your husband, and talking all that negative talk about him, which only puts a curse on him, you might find that God would change his heart toward you also. Negative talking does not improve a negative situation, rather, it reinforces it because it brings with it the presence of evil spirits.

STUDY QUESTIONS

1. Read Acts Chapters 1-5.

2. Memorize Matthew 5:11-12.

3. When was Leah's broken heart healed?

4. How did polygamy come about? Is it scriptural?

5. Why does nagging and complaining produce more harm than good?

CHAPTER FOUR

PRAISE WILL MAKE PROVISION FOR ALL OUR NEEDS

Praise is so powerful because it is the language of creation. It has creative power.

Praise prepares the worm for the bird. When the bird wakes up in the early morning, praising and singing, it causes a worm to wiggle its way up to the surface where it ends up in the belly of the praiser.

I wonder what our menu for the day would be if we woke up singing and praising the Lord.

If we spent as much time praising the Lord as we do worrying about how God is going to meet our needs we would have so much less stress in our lives.

It is a proven fact that many of our sicknesses are caused by stress. In fact, even Christians are suffering because of stress. And we should be free of all stress, for we have a mighty God Who loves us and has saved us from our sins. We know that He is in control of our lives. With Him in charge, everything will turn out all right. Did Jesus not say, "Let not your hearts be troubled..." (John 14:1). Paul added to that, *"Be anxious for nothing: but in every thing, by prayer and supplication WITH THANKSGIVING, let your requests be made known unto God"* (Philippians 4:6).

We are exhorted to praise God when we pray. Praise will banish our fears and unbelief. It will speed the answer on its way to us.

I would like to draw your attention to the verses before and after verse six, *"Rejoice in the Lord always. Again I say, rejoice! Let your moderation be known unto all men. The Lord is at hand. Be anxious for nothing, but in every thing by prayer and supplication, with thanksgiving let your requests be made known unto God; and the peace of God, which surpasses all understanding, shall keep your hearts and minds through Christ Jesus."*

Paul is telling the church at Philippi that they should always make sure that their prayers were accompanied by praises to God. Paul speaks with authority because he had suffered a severe beating and imprisonment there, and had experienced the power of praise in difficult times. He remembers how he and Silas prayed and praised the Lord at midnight when they had been beaten and thrown into the dungeon part of the prison where they lay in pain with their feet in stocks. He remembers how he and his companion praised the Lord together until God sent a great earthquake that broke up the foundations of the prison, sprung the doors wide open and loosed the bands and chains of the prisoners. It was an experience he would never forget. He knew that this miracle had happened because of their praises to God.

When we praise the Lord we release the power of God into action on our behalf. We create vibrations that radiate up to the throne of God and down into the bowels of the earth, vibrations that are so powerful they will cause the earth to quake. They will even destroy the fetters that have held us captive all our lives.

PROVISION IN THE DESERT

In 1961 I visited Israel for the first time. One of the thrills of that unforgettable time was the drive through the Sinai desert from Jerusalem to Eilat. While there we stayed with a Jewish Believer who had miraculously survived Nazi Germany. She was living by faith in what was then a very small city, and nothing at all like it is now.

As I was helping her prepare food in the kitchen one day I noticed a Scripture on the wall above her sink, *"Therefore take no thought, saying, What shall we eat? or, What shall we drink?...for your Heavenly Father knoweth that ye have need of all these things"* (Matthew 6:31-32). Magda (I believe that was her name) told me that many times she did not know where her next meal was coming from, so the Lord had one day given her that verse as a promise that if she would not worry, but trust Him day by day, He would never fail her. He would always feed her. "I don't worry any more since I put that Scripture on the wall, I just praise Him because I know He will provide," she said to me.

I have heard many sermons on faith, but that was not only a sermon, it was an object lesson, and a testimony to the power of God to meet our needs when we stop worrying and start praising the Lord for His provision, even when we do not see the answer.

God does not want us to worry. It grieves His heart when He sees us suffering from fear and worry, and even getting sick over it because of stress.

We must be careful not to offend the Lord by our lack of confidence. For "without faith it is impossible to please God." We want to please Him. Therefore we exercise our faith through praises to Him, and as we praise, our faith grows stronger.

PRAISE OPENS A FOUNTAIN IN THE DESERT

God can not only set up a table in the wilderness, He can also open springs of living water through praise.

For thirty years the Children of Israel had been miraculously supplied with abundant water from a miracle-rock that followed them in the wilderness (1 Corinthians 10:4). But in the fortieth year, after Miriam died, the miracle supply of water suddenly came to an end. God doesn't always do things the same way. This time He was going to teach them the miracle of supply through praise.

The Lord spoke to Moses, "Gather the people together, and I will give them water." When they had assembled, the Lord told Israel to begin singing a song about water, "Spring up O well." The princes of the tribes were commanded to dig in the sand with their staves while all of them, three million voices, rang out in songs of praises to God to a well that they could not see (Numbers 21:16-18).

While they sang their song of praise, a miracle happened; the power of three million people praising the Lord at the same time went up to God in Heaven and down into the bowels of the earth. The vibrations of their anointed faith-song put pressure on the foundations of the earth to such a great degree that suddenly the rocks burst open, and from the depth of the earth a sea of water sprouted up out of the sands like a mighty geyser. It was something like Old Faithful in Yellowstone National Park, USA.

Today it would take machinery costing millions of dollars to dig to such a depth to discover that water. And it would take much time and manpower. But twelve walking canes scratching the sand and the praises of God's people did it all in minutes.

PRAISE SANCTIFIES THE FOOD, AND MAKES IT KOSHER

Having lived in foreign lands for many years I have had to "eat what was set before me, asking no questions for conscience sake" (1 Corinthians 10:27). I must honestly confess that many times I would rather have gone hungry, had I known what was on my plate!

In the days when Paul wrote his letters to Timothy he knew that Timothy was having the same kind of problem, only more so! This was because Timothy had a Jewish mother, and therefore, as far as dietary laws were concerned, he had probably been raised as an observant Jew, although he had not been circumcised until he began to work with Paul in the ministry. This was because his father was Greek (Acts 16:1). Timothy often was sent out on missionary journeys by Paul, or he was left behind to pastor some of the new churches that had sprung up as a result of their ministry in the places where they had preached the Gospel. Many of the new converts were Gentiles who did not observe the dietary laws of the Jews, and Timothy would have had to eat food that was not kosher for a Jew to eat. So Paul had to give him counsel.

In answer to this problem Paul very wisely advises Timothy, *"...in the latter times some shall depart from the faith ... commanding to abstain from meats, which God hath created to be received with thanksgiving of them which believe and know the truth. For every creature of God is good, and nothing to be refused, if it be received with thanksgiving: For it is sanctified by the word of God and prayer"* (1 Timothy 4:3-5).

Paul was saying that whatever we eat, if it is received with praises to God and a thankful heart, is sanctified, and will not bring condemnation upon us.

I have always claimed that the food I eat is sanctified by prayer. In all the years I have served God I cannot remember ever being made ill by what I have eaten, but I have drunk unclean water in India, which I never thought to pray over, and it gave me typhoid fever, which God miraculously healed me of on the fifth day.

Praising God over our food sends healing rays into it, so that we can eat without feeling guilty of sinning against God, or fear of contamination. Of course, if we know that a certain food is dangerous we would be tempting God to eat or drink it. Paul is talking about food that is served us in the homes where we are being entertained, where, to refuse to eat would offend our host and hostess. So the next time you are invited to someone's home for dinner, and they serve a food you do not usually eat, do not feel condemned if you are obliged to partake. Do it with praises in your heart, remembering *"every creature of God is good, and nothing to be refused, if it be received with thanksgiving."*

NEVER GET TIRED OF SAYING "THANK YOU" TO GOD!

Jonathan Rosenblum, in his article, *"Why So Many Mitzvot?"* in The Jerusalem Post, June 16, 2000 writes, "No religion has so many rules governing every aspect of life [as Judaism does], — rules about which shoe to put on first in the morning, about how and what to eat, detailed laws of proper and improper speech. We recite blessings upon rising in the morning and before going to sleep at night, blessings before and after eating, even blessings after going to the bathroom."

Seeing as so many serious diseases begin in the intestines it is a wise thing to thank God for healthy elimination of the bowels. And it is certainly wise to bless God before falling to sleep. I believe it makes for a better rest in the night, and protection during our hours of sleeping. Perhaps we would be in a better mood all day if we would praise the Lord when we first wake up in the morning!

STUDY QUESTIONS

1. Read Exodus 17:1-7; Numbers 20:1-13; and Numbers 21:16-18.

2. Memorize Philippians 4:6.

3. When did praising open a fountain in the deep?

4. How can food be made "kosher?"

5. What else does "praising God, and blessing the food" do for it?

CHAPTER FIVE

PRAISE OPENS THE CLOSED DOORS

Isaiah 60:18 says, *"Violence shall no more be heard in thy land, wasting nor destruction within thy borders; but thou shalt call thy walls Salvation, and thy gates Praise."*

Primarily this is a promise to Israel for the future. But it gives us the secret to the security of Israel. Ever since Israel became a nation in 1948 it has suffered from violence, violence against her embassies abroad, her people, and even violence on her streets. "Intifada" is a word that brings fear to every Israeli heart. But the day will come when violence against God's chosen people will be a thing of the past.

The word "salvation" is *"Yeshuwah"* in Hebrew. The name of Jesus, *"Yeshua"* comes from this word. By this we know that day of security and salvation will come when the people of Israel accept their Saviour, Yeshua, as their Messiah and Lord. When that happens He will guard the borders of Israel. And Israel will not be hemmed in on every side by her enemies because God will open the gates to the nations around them when they learn the power of Praise. Praise will also open the gates of the nations that are barred against Israel now.

As more and more Israelis accept Jesus as their Messiah the nation becomes more and more protected from her enemies, and accepted by the other nations of the world which refuse to recognize her or have anything to do with her.

Have you ever felt as though you were hemmed in on every side, a prisoner of circumstance, from which there was no escape? Maybe your "prison" wasn't a jail cell, but it might just as well have been, because you know in your heart that for you there is no future, no tomorrow, nothing at all to look forward to. Day will follow day, until you think you will die of boredom. The dreams you once had lie in ashes at your feet! You have lost all confidence in yourself. All hope is long gone!

Have you tried the key of praise? Somewhere in your cell there is a door that will open up if you will use that key. The name of the door is PRAISE, and the lettering on the key in your hand is PRAISE. Try it!

PAUL AND SILAS OPENED
THE PRISON DOORS THROUGH PRAISE

Several years ago I had the privilege of visiting the ruins of Philippi where Paul and Silas had first preached in Europe. His first convert was a woman, Lydia, who invited the apostles to stay in her house.

During their ministry in that city Paul was continually accosted on the street by a young woman who was possessed of a spirit of divination who screamed at them, "These men are the servants of the most high God, which shew unto us the way of salvation." Paul was exceedingly grieved because he didn't want any demon advertising his ministry, or doing his Public Relations work. So he commanded the demon to leave her at once. When that happened she lost her ability to tell fortunes and make money for her owners who had used her as a slave for their personal gain. In anger against Paul and Silas they brought lying accusations against them and had them severely beaten and thrown into prison.

Paul, being a Roman citizen, could have gotten these men into big trouble, instead, he and Silas prayed and sang praises unto God, which all the prisoners heard because it was midnight and all was quiet.

While they were praising the Lord, "suddenly there was a great earthquake, so that the foundations of the prison were shaken: and immediately all the doors were opened, and every one's bands were loosed."

Praising the Lord, not only opened the doors, it also broke the chains and fetters that were fastened to the limbs of all of the prisoners. Every one of them could have escaped in the darkness of the night. But Paul's commanding presence kept them all in perfect order. The jailor was saved, and all his house. And Paul celebrated a "midnight-mass" with the family after baptizing them all down at the river where Lydia had been baptized earlier (Acts 16).

PRAISE RELEASES THE ANOINTING THAT BREAKS THE YOKE

Isaiah, the great prophet of Israel, said, *"And it shall come to pass in that day, that his burden shall be taken away from off thy shoulder, and his yoke from off thy neck, and the yoke shall be destroyed because of the anointing"* (Isaiah 10:27).

Although I was a missionary, serving the Lord in China, for years I felt as though I was in bondage. I could not find fulfillment in the work that I was doing.

Many times I felt so burdened with the sight of the great harvest fields of lost souls which I seemed to have no way of reaping. I remember singing the beautiful old missionary hymn, *"Let me burn out for Thee, oh Lord,"* with the tears rolling down my cheeks. But my days were spent in the same kind of work I would have done as a housewife and mother back home. After a while I was invited to conduct the choir of one of the large churches in Hong Kong; I even played the Hammond Organ, and now and then taught a small Chinese Sunday School class. I did midwifery, together with another missionary. That was fun, and exciting, but it did not fulfill the calling and destiny that was on my life.

Over and over again, as I cried out to God, I heard the Scripture deep in my soul, *"The Yoke shall be destroyed by the anointing."* I didn't know it was for me. I thought the Holy Spirit was referring to my husband getting the anointing, so that our calling could be fulfilled together.

But I was wrong! It was for ME! God led me into a twenty-one day fast, and a mighty new anointing fell upon my life. Every yoke of bondage and fear was broken in me, and I began to preach the Gospel as I never had before. I preached in English and in Chinese, and later, even in German. I picked up my accordion and began to write songs of praise and worship to God. I carried that accordion around the world into over one hundred nations, singing and preaching and teaching the nations. Praise had broken the terrible yoke that had kept me a prisoner of circumstances for so many years. I was free to be what God has made me to be.

This is the message I try to teach God's daughters today. Many are waiting for someone else to get the anointing, while God is waiting for them. Those "prison doors" will burst wide open, and you will begin a soul-saving ministry that is greater than you ever dreamed, if you will only begin to praise the Lord, and then obey Him when He sends that "earthquake" that will shake the foundation of your lifestyle, and open the door for you to escape the fetters that hold your feet in stocks, many of which have been your own doing.

Some of you have placed your own selves into bondage. You have no one else to blame but yourself. You acted in haste, and of your life, you have made waste. But all is not lost if, in the midnight hour of your soul, you will cry out to God, and spare not. Start now to praise Him, and watch for the doors that will spring open "of their own accord."

STUDY QUESTIONS

1. Read Acts 16:1-40.

2. Memorize Isaiah 10:27.

3. What happened with Paul and Silas praised the Lord?

4. Wherein lies the true security of Israel's borders?

5. How does praise break the yoke?

CHAPTER SIX

PRAISE BRINGS REVIVAL

In Acts 2:46-47 we can discover the key to the Early Church Revival. *"And they, continuing daily with one accord in the temple, and breaking bread from house to house, did eat their meat with gladness and singleness of heart, Praising God, and having favour with all the people. And the Lord added to the church daily such as should be saved."*

Praising the Lord brought revival, which brought joy, which caused the people to praise the Lord still more, which brings still greater revival, etc. Oh, if God's people would only begin to praise the Lord! I wonder how great a revival would break out upon the Church around the world!

The late Rev. Reg Layzell, pastor of Glad Tidings Temple, Vancouver, Canada, tells how revival began at the beginning of his ministry. I would like to quote from his excellent book, "Unto Perfection."

He tells how he was invited to hold special meetings in a small church in Abbotsford, British Columbia. The pastor was ill, and not expected to live, so the meetings were turned over to him. He was not an experienced preacher and certainly did not consider himself to be an evangelist. He says, "I stumbled and perspired my way through the morning service. I was embarrassed, and I am sure the people were not at all impressed with the great evangelist. The meeting Sunday night was rather ordinary, and I was thankful when it was all over. If the Pastor had not been sick I would have gone to him and said, 'Look, I made a mistake. This is not the call of God, and I am going home.' That would have been the end of that, for I still had my return ticket. Tuesday night there were only about twenty-five people present for a very poor meeting. I thought to myself that this just will not do; either God had to answer or I was going home. I decided to spend all day Wednesday fasting. I told the pastor's wife I would not be in all day. I was going to stay in the church and would be fasting. I took some water to the church and started my fast. I groaned all morning in a little room off in the corner. I did everything in my power to get God to 'feel sorry for me.' I did everything in groaning prayer, and the Heavens were brass. Have you ever tried to get God's sympathy? God is at times most unsympathetic! He does not respond to self-pity. God only responds to faith. He knows the answer, for He knows what is in the Word.

"As I was praying, a Scripture came to my mind. Psalm 22:3, *'But thou art holy, O Thou that inhabitest the praises of Israel.'* Immediately I knew God was challenging me or convicting me. I thought of every sin I had ever committed, and repented, and still the Heavens were brass. There was no deliverance in repentance. I was just repeating the many sins God had already forgiven and forgotten. It didn't work. Then the rest of the Scripture began to grip me, *'O Thou that inhabitest the praises of Israel.'* It began to click. He lives in the praises of His people. I needed God that day, and I thought, 'If this verse is true, then I will fill this building with God.' So around 3.00 p.m. I began to praise the Lord loudly! 'Praise the Lord! Glory to God! Hallelujah!'

"I walked around the piano, I walked around every pew in the building, up and down, with my hands in the air praising the Lord loudly. I went into the washrooms, the cloakroom, the furnace room. I spent until 7:15 p.m. just walking into every niche and corner of the building. At 7:15 p.m. two people came in, so I dropped to my knees at the platform.

"Prior to this time we had praised in the prayer room, but never in the open church. We had never offered the 'sacrifice of praise.' So I quietly continued to praise the Lord. Then the meeting was started, and I announced the hymn, 'There is Power in the Blood.' I will always remember that. We sang the first verse, the second verse, and then the chorus. Suddenly a girl on one side of the church threw her hands up and began to speak in tongues. About five minutes later a sister on the other side began to shout and speak in tongues. Then someone in the centre aisles did the same. They were baptized in the Holy Ghost! This was the first time I had ever seen anyone baptized in the Holy Ghost in a public meeting during the song service. Thus was born the message of praise, which is the secret of continuous revival. He lives in the praises of His people!

"As a result, instead of going back to the business world, I came into full-time ministry on the west coast of Canada."

Praising the Lord brings the Presence of the Lord down among His people. This is because the Lord dwells in the environment of praise. Heaven is filled with the praises of the saints and the angels. When we praise the Lord on earth, we bring a little bit of Heaven down upon this world. This makes God "feel at home" here on earth.

It also makes the angels "feel at home." The angels are happy when we praise the Lord. They draw nigh to listen and, if we could see them, we would be amazed how they join in with us when we praise the Lord.

Hebrews 12:1 tells us that we are "compassed about with a great cloud of witnesses." These witnesses are the angels and the saints who have lived before us. They are the unseen hosts who are praying for us in Heaven, and the prophets of yesterday who desire to "look into" our activities, hoping and praying that we will be faithful to the final works of God, and the ushering in of the Kingdom of God. Let us not fail them. They paid such a great price to give us the truths that we hold dear to our hearts today. Many laid down their lives as martyrs so that we might have our Bibles. Some, like William Tyndale, were even burned at the stake for making the Bible available to God's people in the English language. They are concerned that we do not fail the Lord after all that.

STUDY QUESTIONS

1. Read Acts chapters 11-15.

2. Memorize Acts 2:46-47.

3. What act of man played an important part in the Latter Rain Revival?

4. Who is watching us?

5. Why are they concerned for us?

CHAPTER SEVEN

WHEN OUR PRAYERS ARE ACCOMPANIED WITH PRAISE WE CAN COME IMMEDIATELY INTO GOD'S PRESENCE

When John, the writer of Revelation had a vision of Heaven he saw the true, fulfillment of worship as it actually takes place at the Throne of God. Everything that God instructed Moses to do and to teach Aaron, in regard to the ritual of worship, was only a pattern of the Heavenly. This is what John saw:

In Revelation 8:3-4 we read, *"Then another angel, having a golden censer, came and stood at the altar. He was given much incense, that he should offer it with the prayers of all the saints upon the golden altar which was before the throne. And the smoke of the incense, with the prayers of the saints, ascended before God from the angel's hand."*

Leviticus 16:2-3 *"And the LORD said unto Moses, Speak unto Aaron thy brother, that he come not at all times into the holy place within the vail before the mercy seat, which is upon the ark; that he die not: for I will appear in the cloud (of incense) upon the mercy seat. Thus shall Aaron come into the holy place: with a young bullock for a sin offering, and a ram for a burnt offering."*

Leviticus 16:12-14 *"And he shall take a censer full of burning coals of fire from off the altar (the brazen altar where the sacrifices were made), before the LORD, and his hands full of sweet incense beaten small, and bring it within the vail: And he shall put the incense upon the fire before the LORD, that the cloud of the incense may cover the mercy seat that is upon the testimony, that he die not: And he shall take of the blood of the bullock, and sprinkle it with his finger upon the mercy seat eastward; and before the mercy seat shall he sprinkle of the blood with his finger seven times."*

The High Priest could only enter the Holy of Holies, behind the veil that separated it from the Holy Place, once a year. Before he entered, he was commanded to place incense upon the coals of fire that were in a golden incense censer on the Table of Incense in the Holy Place. After the scented smoke filled the Tabernacle, and covered the Mercy Seat, Aaron would bring the blood of the sacrificed ram into the Holy of Holies where it was sprinkled on the Ark of the Covenant, and on the sides of it. Without the sacrificial blood, and the holy cloud of incense, he dared not approach God's Holy Presence.

In the thirteenth verse we read that Aaron had to put the incense on the fire before the Lord, that the cloud of incense would cover the mercy seat. He was warned that if this ritual was not strictly observed he would fall down, dead.

We cannot over emphasize the importance of the fact that it was only AFTER the smoke from the incense filled the Holy of Holies that the High Priest could approach the Presence of God, and be able to sprinkle the blood of atonement on and before the Mercy Seat. If he disobeyed this law, he would die. And, just in case he forgot, bells were sewed into the hem of his garment so that the people could tell by their ringing that the priest was still alive.

Rev. John Gomes, in his beautiful teaching on the subject of praise, explains that, since the death of Jesus, coals of fire that are burning the sweet incense no longer have to be taken from the Altar of Incense in order to enter behind the Veil into the Holy of Holies. Today our praises (which the cloud of incense symbolizes) go before us into the Presence of God, making it possible for us to approach the High and Holy One Who Sits upon His Throne. The earthly Altar of Incense was the symbol of the sacrifice of praise offered up to God by the saints on earth, which ascends on high, and spreads its fragrance to all of Heaven from the true Altar of Incense which, even now, stands before the Heavenly Mercy Seat, the Throne of God, where John saw it in Heaven.

The veil (the sins of our flesh) that separated us from the Holy of Holies (God's Presence) was taken away by the Lord's broken body. So when we praise the Lord, we, like David, obtain the mercies of God. Let us praise Him so that we can come directly into God's presence.

After David had brought the Ark of the Covenant to Jerusalem he placed into a tent-tabernacle he had made for it which is called "The Tabernacle of David" today. It was only a temporary abode for this very holy object.

Now, we know that David was not perfect, nor sinless. In fact he himself confessed that God would not let him build the Temple because of his sins. (1 Kings 5:3; 2 Samuel 7;1-8; 1 Chronicles 22:7-11).

Yet, in spite of his imperfections, and that he was of the tribe of Judah, who had no authority to come into the Presence of the Ark, he entered into the

Tabernacle which he had erected, sat before the Lord, and worshipped him — and was not struck dead! (2 Samuel 7:18)

This could only have happened because he was a praiser. Praise alone, protected him from the vengeance that fell on anyone who dared to come into God's Presence unlawfully. David's life of praise qualified him to cause God to hold the golden scepter of acceptance out to him. It was the "cloud of sweet incense" that covered all his failures, so that God only heard the sweet minstrel of Israel's song of the Lord, and forgot to remember his transgressions.

PRAISE USHERS US INTO HIS COURTS

Psalm 100:4 is a wonderful verse in the Bible, *"Enter into His gates with thanksgiving, and into His courts with praise: be thankful unto Him, and bless His name."*

These are three ways of expressing gratitude: thanksgiving, praise, and blessing His name! It is an all-out expression of the soul which ushers us straight into the Presence of God. It is the way to the Throne Room.

We all long to be ushered into the Throne Room of Heaven. But if we never visit it while we are here on earth, how can we ever think that we will qualify to visit it after we die! We will not love Him more then, than what we love Him now. If we worship and praise Him now, we are preparing for Throne Room Ministry and Worship, both in this world and in the world to come.

We must understand that there is a difference between praise and worship. Praise is the expression of thankfulness, while worship is the expression of adoration. I can praise you for your good cooking, your beautiful piano playing, etc, but I can never worship you. However, praise is important, because it opens the Throne Room of Heaven to us, so that we can come into the Divine Presence of God, Himself. It prepares our hearts with the right attitude, so that we are capable of true worship. And once we are there, we can truly worship Him. Praise is the elevator that lifts us from earth's sphere to Heavenly spheres. Praise is the door, the Beautiful Gate that leads to the Temple of God.

Praise is the power behind the thrust that launches us beyond the limitations of earthly gravity, into the unlimited dimensions of outer space.

Grumbling, murmuring, complaining, moaning will only keep you earth-bound. It has not power to thrust you free from your circumstances. Instead, the wrong kind of attitude will only aggravate your already negative circumstances. So, I challenge you, in Jesus Name, Break Free With Praises.

STUDY QUESTIONS

1. Read Leviticus 16:1-34, Revelation 8:1-5.

2. Memorize Psalm 100:4.

3. What was the cloud of incense in the Tabernacle a type of?

4. Why was David, who was not a Levite, nor a priest able to sit before the Ark of the Covenant when all others were forbidden to come near. Why was he not smitten dead?

5. What two important things allow us to approach the Presence of God today?

CHAPTER EIGHT

THE SACRIFICE OF PRAISE

Psalm 107:22 says, *"Let them sacrifice the sacrifices of thanksgiving, and declare His works with rejoicing."* God is pleased when we show Him gratitude for all His goodness to us.

In Deuteronomy 8:10 God says, *"When thou hast eaten and art full, then thou shalt bless the Lord thy God for the good land which He hath given thee."* Praise is the expression of a thankful heart that is filled with gratitude.

God's people are so ungrateful. We never seem to remember to be thankful for all His benefits. We take so much for granted. That is why it is a "sacrifice" for us to praise the Lord. We feel more like grumbling, than what we feel like praising. We would rather complain than be thankful.

The Children of Israel were commanded to bring the Sacrifice of Praise. Today, we too bring the "Sacrifice of Praise," the fruit of our lips. Hebrews 13:15, *"Therefore by Him let us continually offer the sacrifice of praise to God, that is, the fruit of our lips, giving thanks to His name."*

It really should not be a "sacrifice" for us to praise the Lord. We should want to praise Him, but we are all guilty of neglecting to praise Him. Shame on us!

We have so much more to praise the Lord for than the Children of Israel because we have an eternal inheritance through Jesus Christ. Colossians 1:12 says,

"Giving thanks unto the Father, which hath made us meet to be partakers of the inheritance of the saints in light." Colossians 2:7 says that we should *"abound with thanksgiving."*

In 1 Peter 2:9 we read, *"But ye are a chosen generation, a royal priesthood, a holy nation, a peculiar people; that ye should shew forth the praises of Him who hath called you out of darkness into His marvelous light:"* Just thinking of who we are, and what our calling is should cause us to shout out the glorious praises of God. Our calling is, not only to praise, but to show the praises of God, i.e. to give honour and glory to God through our lives.

WHEN IS "OFFERING THE SACRIFICE OF PRAISE" A TRUE SACRIFICE?

When is praising the Lord a true "sacrifice of praise?"

I used to think that if we praise the Lord when we do not feel like it that we are bringing Him the "sacrifice of praise." But now I believe it is more than praising Him when we feel grumpy, or depressed, or angry about something. It is praising God when the heart is truly broken, when you stand at the grave of a loved one, or when the doctor tells you that you have cancer, or after waiting and praying to have a baby you have a miscarriage, or you find your baby is born with Downs Syndrome, or you have just been fired from your job, or your unwed daughter is pregnant, or your son tells you he is gay, or you find your husband has a secret lover, or your wife tells you she wants a divorce, or your granddaughter has disappeared and you don't know if she has run away from home or been abducted, or you have to declare bankruptcy, or you stand by helplessly while you watch your house burn down, or beloved members of your family have been killed in a terrible crash, or you discover your mother has Alzheimer's Disease! When things like that happen, and you can still praise God, even with the tears running down your cheeks you are offering to God a true "sacrifice of praise."

PRAISING GOD WHEN TRIED BY FIRE

In November, 1990 we had a terrible fire in Engeltal, our ministry headquarters in Arkansas. In one night we lost our administration building with everything in it. Practically nothing in it was saved. The fire took our offices, our office machinery, computers, printers, typesetters, printing presses, book store, warehouse that had about $100,000 in books and supplies, our Audio Tapes, Video tapes, Bible School, book store, musical instruments — everything! We lost it all in one night. And we had no insurance!

We stood on the top of the hill, looking down on the valley, watching it burn, not knowing if the rest of the buildings would also go up in flame. The tears were running down my cheeks. My husband was down at the fire; together with a few helpers he was trying to keep it from spreading. If it did we would lose our home and all the ministry houses and buildings. It already was an almost two million dollar loss.

The night was icy cold, so someone drove me to our neighbours home. We woke them up, it was about 2 or 3 in the morning. Pitch dark. When we told them the shocking news we all sat dazed, in the living room. Inside of me, I heard a song, "Blessed be the name, Blessed be the name, Blessed be the name of the Lord!" I asked Dorothy to go to the piano and play that dear old chorus. When she began, we all sat back, raised our hands to Heaven and sang unto the Lord, "Blessed be the Name of the Lord!" We sang it and sang it. It calmed my soul, it brought the Comforter close by, it lifted me up from the suffering into the sublime. I could cope with my terrible trial because God was bigger than my tragedy.

Rev. Carl Hahn, in his Journal, "Awakened By An Angel" tells about a pair of finches that live on their front porch.

One day he saw them start to try to build a nest on their porch. The spot they selected was a small ledge on top of a post supporting the porch roof. Every day they brought in some twigs and things, but the nest materials always slipped off the edge onto the floor of the porch. There was always a mess of things to sweep from the porch. After four weeks of failure for these two little birds he began to feel sorry for them. So he drove a couple of small nails on the edge of the ledge.

It took the happy singing pair of finches about three days to build a nest. A little while after that he saw the female bird sitting on the nest, and the male bird bringing food to her. He knew she had started to lay her eggs. But a short while later he saw the bird nest with two broken eggs on the floor of their porch. Evidently some other bird, probably a blue jay, had destroyed the nest. Then he saw the female finch trying to keep two more eggs from falling off the ledge, but eventually they also fell out. When Carl and his wife came home from church one Sunday afternoon they did not see nor hear any happy singing finches. He writes:

"I was somewhat saddened, seeing this disastrous event for the pair of finches, yet I knew Jesus taught in Matthew 10:29 that what happens to the birds is within our Father's will."

The Holy Spirit spoke to him and said, "There have been times and events, and there will continue to be times and events when it appears to some that Our Father is not in control of the time nor the event that happens to a human being. When you, as a Born Again Christian, find yourself in such a situation, believing for a miracle is not the only alternative you have. Even though you find yourself in a situation in which it appears to some that Our Father is not involved, if you keep on believing, and having faith in Our Father, at some point in time you will see evidence that Our Father is working concerning your situation. Keep this important truth in mind. If you are in such a situation, and you pray, if Our Father does not respond with some type of miracle, after the event is over, you will always find yourself to be a more mature Born Again Christian."

The Holy Spirit showed him how an angel was involved in what had happened and told him why, "It was because, there are some people who believe that if Our Father does not respond with some type of miracle of deliverance, they have missed the will of Our Father. Though miracles are wonderful, and are the basis of many great testimonies, the truth of the matter is that there is a type of spiritual maturity which can only result from a born again Christian journeying through some difficult times. This is a prophetic message which still needs to be heard."

He added, "When a born again Christian goes through a hard and difficult experience I (the Holy Spirit) will so lead the person that the result will be a more meaningful and happier life. When a person, who is not a born again Christian, goes through a hard and difficult experience, Satan will try to use the event to destroy that person."

Rev. Hahn said the parable of the event was still not totally complete. Ten days after the birds' nest was destroyed, on Mother's Day, they started to rebuild their nest. They were again singing happily as they worked. When it was complete the female finch sat on her nest hatching her second nest of eggs. Rev. Hahn was still trying to correlate this teaching of the Holy Spirit in his understanding and the teaching of some Christians who say we can live in *divine health* to such an extent that we will not be sick.

Rev. Hahn continues, "Almost two weeks later, my wife and I noticed that the female finch was no longer sitting on her nest of eggs on our front porch. Upon closer examination it became apparent that the nest had again been robbed. When I began to think about how this was the second time this pair of finch's nest had been robbed this spring I began to notice that I had an unanswered question in my mind. My question was, "If Our Father really does know when a bird falls to the ground why would He permit a pair of finch's to go through this experience two times in one spring?" This was not a very troubling thought for me, so I did not really give my question very much consideration.

"The following morning Precious (his guardian angel) woke me up at 4:10 A.M. and told me to listen. Outside it was still more dark than it was daylight. When I listened I heard one songbird beginning to sing. Precious awakened me again at 5:10 A.M., and then I heard several songbirds singing.

"Angel Precious said to me, 'You probably will not see the pair of finches on your porch today, but they are singing. When Our Father created song birds He put a song within them to sing. Even though the pair of finches experienced the type of thing you humans call a tragedy, the pair of finches have not lost their song. They are still singing.'"*

THEREFORE WE NEED TO TRUST IN HIM AT ALL TIMES

Perhaps one reason God permitted this tragedy to happen was that we all might learn the lesson of the "sacrifice of praise." The finches had no "bitterness" against God for the tragic loss of their "home" and children. They still could praise the Lord.

Oh, but you say, "They can't love like I do! They cannot feel the pain like I do!"

I would ask you what would you call the sacrifice a mother bird makes to sit, hour after hour on her eggs, not eating, unless she is fed, never leaving her nest, no matter what? If that isn't love, what is love?

---

* For a full detail of Rev. Carl Hahn's experiences see the order form at the back of this book.

God wants us to have such confidence in Him that even though things do not work out like we think they should, we can trust in Him that He knows what is best. He has the long-range plan.

One of the most amazing admonitions is, *"In every thing give thanks: for this is the will of God in Christ Jesus concerning you"* (1 Thessalonians 5:18).

Many of God's people are deeply troubled about their life's circumstances. They cannot find peace in days of trials and testings. This is because they do not know Colossians 3:15, *"...Let the peace of God rule in your hearts, to the which also ye are called in one body; and be thankful."* When we are thankful to God, and try to see His will, even through a veil of tears, we can have His peace in our hearts.

Are you troubled today? Is there a storm in your life? I beg you to rest your case in the hands of God. Let Him decide what is best for you.

On the night when Jesus was arrested in the Garden He wrestled with great prayers until He was able to commit everything to His Father. When He prayed, *"...nevertheless not my will, but Thine, be done,"* Jesus was released of His fears and entered into a state of perfect peace. Nothing could shake His confidence, His peace, His trust in the Father's will, in spite of the torment and suffering that He had to go through. And when you come to that place of trust and commitment the peace of God, such as you have never known, will enter your heart also. And that peace will bring joy and comfort to your soul.

STUDY QUESTIONS

1. Read Acts Chapters 16-20.

2. Memorize Hebrews 13:15.

3. To whom was the promise given that they are a chosen generation, and royal priesthood and a holy nation?

4. When is the sacrifice of praise a true sacrifice?

5. What lesson did you learn about the pair of finches?

CHAPTER NINE
PRAISE DEFEATS DEMONIC POWERS AND DRIVES AWAY DEMONS

When King Saul deliberately disobeyed the Lord's commands the Spirit of the Lord departed from him, and an evil spirit troubled him. His servants were very concerned. They said, *"Behold now, an evil spirit from God troubleth thee. Let our Lord now command thy servants, which are before thee to seek out a man, who is a cunning (gifted) player on harp, and it shall come to pass, when the evil spirit from God is upon thee, that he shall play with his hand, and thou shalt be well"* 1 Samuel 16:15-16.

King Saul agreed to it, and they sent for David, the son of Jesse. The Bible says that when David played with his hand the evil spirit that was upon Saul departed from him and he was refreshed. One translation renders it that he was "delivered, made whole" (1 Samuel 16:4-23).

We can be sure that David played the psalms of praises which the Lord had given him as he had herded his father's flocks in the Shepherds fields of Bethlehem. Many a long night David had worshipped the Lord and sung His praises as he suffered through the cold of the wintry seasons, and the dangers of the wild animals, such as the lions and the bears (1 Samuel 17:36). He knew that through praising the Lord he could conquer ferocious beasts, great giants, like Goliath, and evil spirits.

Have some of your family members opened themselves up to demon spirits through their sinful way of life? Have they brought demons into your home? If you will begin to praise the Lord, you will drive those demons out of your house. Ask God to give you a song that will meet the need.

Rev. Grace McGonigle tells a story of how, when her children were small and her days filled with tending to their needs, she discovered that awaking in the middle of night gave her the best opportunity for studying the Bible. This became her habit for years. One evening as she awakened to study her Bible she was surprised to hear, aloud, as though it were played on a radio, a song. She immediately wrote down the music notes. When she had written the music the words for the song were given to her by the Holy Spirit. They just flowed out, and in a short time they were completed. She had a strong feeling that this was a song like David played on his harp when the evil spirits vexed Saul, as recorded in 1 Samuel 16:23. Later a word of prophecy was given to her that this was the actually song that David had played when the evil spirit had vexed the soul of Saul.

It is possible for the Holy Spirit to give us lost melodies and lost poetry. Beautiful gemstones out of antiquity.

Satan hates to hear people praise the Lord. The demons cannot stand in the presence of one who is praising God from his heart. Put the enemy to flight with loud praises.

Apparently, King Saul's deliverance was only temporary. He was never totally delivered. The evil spirits came back on him again and again because they were not cast out. We can only read of such deliverance taking place in the New Testament. But he did have respite from them until he would allow the spirit of jealousy against David to get ahold of him, and then they would come back to torment him. And there was no relief, for David was the object of his hatred, and he tried to kill him. After that David did not dare to try to minister to Saul.

Today, we have the Lord Jesus' command to cast out demons in His name, but David lived under the Old Covenant.

PRAISE BRINGS VICTORY IN THE TIME OF BATTLE

Strategy in warfare is one of the most important aspects of winning the battle. Great nations, like the United States have entire military academies dedicated to the purpose of training young men to serve their country. Some of the most well-known are the U.S. Merchant Marine Academy at Kings Point, N.Y.; Army Academy at West Point, N.Y.; Air Force Academy at Colorado Springs, CO; Coast Guard Academy at New London, CT; Navy and Marine Corps Academy, Annapolis MD; These all are Federal Academies.

Not one of them trains their soldiers in the type of military warfare that we read about in the Bible. God's strategies are high above ours, even as His wisdom is high above ours. Let us look into one of the most amazing military tactics. We first read about it in Joshua 6:7-20. The results were one hundred percent successful, the city of Jericho fell without the loss of one Israelite soldier.

WHEN JOSHUA FIT THE BATTLE OF JERICHO

When Joshua fit the battle of Jericho the Lord instructed him to march around the walls of the city for seven days. The amazing thing was that on the final time around the priests were commanded to lead the entire army of marchers. At Joshua's command, "Shout, for the Lord hath given you the city,"the priests blew their shofars and the people shouted with a "great" shout. In that instant the city walls collapsed, and the soldiers took the city that day. There was no need for door-to-door combat for the city, as usually happens in city-wars. The shout of Praise and the blowing of the shofars gave the victory.

THE CHOIR LEADS THE ARMY IN THE BATTLE

When good King Jehoshaphat was king over Judah they were suddenly invaded by the Moabites, Ammonites and Edomites. Jehoshaphat set himself to seek the Lord, and proclaimed a fast throughout the land. All Judah gathered together for one great prayer meeting. The result was that the Lord directed him to appoint singers unto the Lord who would *"praise the beauty of holiness, as they went out before the army, and to say, Praise the Lord; for his mercy endureth for ever"* (2 Chronicles 20:21).

The result was tremendous, for as they began to sing and to praise, the Lord set ambushment against the invaders. The men of the three different nations were thrown into confusion; they turned against each other, destroying one another down to the last man.

Such is the power of praising the Lord in battle.

During the last World War I remember a popular song we sang in Canada, "Praise the Lord, and pass the ammunition!" This song was written by Frank Loesser (1910-1969). Rumors were that it was based on the same words, spoken by a Christian sailor by the name of William Maquire (1890-1953), who was waiting for someone to pass him the shells for the ship's canons when they were under attack from an enemy ship. If anyone knows the story, please share it with us.

Psalm 68 gives us the Lord's tactics for warfare, *"The singers went before, the players on instruments followed after; among them were the damsels playing with timbrels"* (Psalm 68:25).

When you find yourself the target of an unexpected attack from the enemy who is trying to destroy you from two or three different directions and ways, I challenge you to start praising the Lord. That will clear the air for the Heavenly Invasion Hosts to sweep down from the Military Academy of Glory and cause your enemy such confusion that he will end up destroying himself. Try Praise!

When Jerusalem was under siege in the days of King Hezekiah and the situation looked hopeless, God called out the women to praise the Lord for victory through laughter, and when the Daughters of Zion "laughed in the Spirit" at the cruel taunts of the enemy, the angel of the Lord slew 185 thousand enemy troops in one night (Isaiah 37:22,36).

STUDY QUESTIONS

1. Read 1 Samuel chapters 13-18; 19-20; Joshua 5:13-6:27; 2 Chronicles 20:1-30.

2. Memorize 2 Chronicles 20:21; Psalm 68:25.

3. Why did an evil spirit torment King Saul, and what eased his suffering?

4. What caused the Walls of Jericho to fall?

5. Describe the battle that took place in the days of King Jehoshaphat.

CHAPTER TEN

THE IMPORTANCE OF
MUSICAL INSTRUMENTS IN PRAISE

All of our talents are given to us by God. And yet, some people feel that it is wrong to play a musical instrument in the House of the Lord.

The reason they take this stand is because the inventor of musical instruments was a descendent of Cain, the man who killed his brother, Abel, and was therefore marked by mankind as evil.

Genesis 4:19-22 says, *"And Lamech took unto him two wives: the name of the one was Adah, and the name of the other Zillah. And Adah bare Jabal: he was the father of such as dwell in tents, and of such as have cattle. And his brother's name was Jubal: he was the father of all such as handle the harp and organ. And Zillah, she also bare Tubalcain, an instructor of every artificer in brass and iron:"*

If it is wrong to play a musical instrument because the man who invented it was a descendant of Cain, then it is wrong to be associated with tents and cattle, or to work with brass and iron because all three inventors of these three things were brothers who were descendants of Cain.

We must remember that it is not the musical instrument that is evil, it is the type of music that is played through it or on it. A musical instrument that is dedicated to God is the same as a life that is given to God. It can be pure and holy, or it can become defiled, and cause others to sin. We do not throw a man out of the church because he is a sinner, nor should we destroy a musical instrument because it has been used to play music that does not glorify God.

I like to think that we ourselves are instruments in the hands of the Great Musician. He can use our lives to make beautiful music.

Rabindranath Tagore (1861-1941), the great Bengali Poet, who won the Nobel Prize for Literature in 1913, in his beautiful collection of Poems called Gitanjali, included a poem that has always deeply stirred my heart. A part of it goes like this:

"This little flute of a reed thou hast carried over hills and dales, and hast breathed through it melodies eternally new. At the immortal touch of thy hands my little heart loses its limits in joy and gives birth to utterance ineffable. Thy infinite gifts come to me only on these very small hands of mine. Ages pass, and still thou pourest, and still there is room to fill."

We are likened to instruments in the hands of a great and infinite God who created us to be an eternal instrument of music in His hands.

KING DAVID USED MUSICAL INSTRUMENTS FOR TEMPLE WORSHIP

King David knew and appreciated the true value of musical instruments. The rabbis tell us that he invented many musical instruments, which he instructed the musicians to play during Temple Worship.

1 Chronicles 15:16 says, *"David told the chief Levites to appoint their brethren the singers, with instruments of music — harps, lyres and cymbals — to play loudly and lift up their voices with joy."*

I Chronicles 16:39-42 tells us that God commanded that musical instruments were to be played during the time that sacrifices were offered up to the Lord upon the altar of burnt offering continually, morning and evening — *"And with them Heman and Jeduthun, and the rest that were chosen, who were expressed by name, to give thanks to the LORD, because his mercy endureth for ever; And with them Heman and Jeduthun with trumpets and cymbals for those that should sound aloud, and instruments for accompanying the songs of God."*

It is interesting to know that it was while the precious lambs were dying as sacrifices for the sins of the people that the last sound those poor things heard was the high praises of the people of God as they were worshipping the Lord. I wonder, did it make their suffering and their death easier for them to bear? Do martyrs hear the choirs of Heaven sing when they die?

I once prayed for a woman who had died to be raised from the dead. When she was restored again she told me that during her "near death experience" she had heard the most beautiful music, and she was very happy. But she heard my voice calling her to come back, and she was brought back into her body. This happened while we were on tour in Rome, Italy. The lady was a member of our tour group.

When David was old, he made his son, Solomon, king over Israel. The Bible says he assembled all the leaders together. He appointed the Levites who were thirty years old and older to their Temple ministry.

There were 38,000. He appointed 24,000 to oversee the work of the house of the Lord, and 6,000 to be officers and judges; 4,000 were gatekeepers, and 4,000 were ordained to praise the Lord with the instruments which David said he had made for praising the Lord (1 Chronicles 23:1-5).

Psalm 150 lists many different instruments that were used for Temple Worship and Praise:

Praise ye the LORD. Praise God in his sanctuary: praise him in the firmament of his power. Praise him for his mighty acts: praise him according to his excellent greatness. Praise him with the sound of the <u>trumpet</u>: praise him with the <u>psaltery</u> and <u>harp</u>. Praise him with the <u>timbrel</u> and dance: praise him with <u>stringed instruments</u> and <u>organs</u>. Praise him upon the <u>loud cymbals</u>: praise him upon the <u>high sounding cymbals.</u> Let every thing that hath breath praise the LORD. Praise ye the LORD."

In 1 Chronicles 25 we can read about the ritual of Temple Worship. It is very interesting. The Amplified Translation renders it, *"Also David and the chiefs of the host of the Lord separated to the temple service some of the sons of <u>Asaph, Heman, and Jeduthun,</u> who should prophesy being inspired with lyres, harps, cymbals. The list of the musicians according to their service was:*

Of the sons of <u>Asaph</u>: Zaccur, Joseph, Nathaniah, and Asharelah, the sons of Asaph, under the direction of Asaph, who prophesied (witnessed and testified under divine inspiration) in keeping with the king's order.

Of the sons of <u>Jeduthun</u>: Gedaliah, Zeri, Jeshaiah, Shimei, Hashabiah, and Mattithiah, six in all, under the direction of their father Jeduthun, who witnessed and prophesied under divine inspiration with the lyre in thanksgiving and praise to the Lord.

Of <u>Heman</u>: the sons of Heman: Bukkiah, Mattaniah, Uzziel, Shebuel, Jerimoth, Hananiah, Hannani, Eliathah, Giddalti, Romamti-ezer, Joshbekashah, Mallothi Hothir, Mahazzioth.

All these were the sons of Heman, the king's seer his mediator, in the words and things of God to exalt Him; for God gave to Heman fourteen sons and three daughters, All of whom were in the choir under the direction of their father for song in the house of the Lord, with cymbals, harps, and lyres for the service of the house of God"

In 2 Chronicles 5:12-14 we read, *"Also the Levites which were the singers, all of them of Asaph, of Heman, of Jeduthun, with their sons and their brethren, being arrayed in white linen, having cymbals and psalteries and harps, stood at the east end of the altar, and with them an hundred and twenty priests sounding with trumpets: It came even to pass, as the trumpeters and singers were as one, to make one sound to be heard in praising and thanking the LORD; and when they lifted up their voice with the trumpets and cymbals and instruments of musick, and praised the LORD, saying, For he is good; for his mercy endureth for ever: that then the house was filled with a cloud, even the house of the LORD; So that the priests could not stand to minister by reason of the cloud: for the glory of the LORD had filled the house of God."*

How beautiful they must have been in their robes of white! Their part in Temple Worship was so important that God registers their names in the Bible. Of the 4000 musicians 288 were very talented singers who had the gifts of playing and singing prophetic songs of praise that were inspired by the Holy Spirit. It was like a little bit of Heaven come down. The Glory was so great that the priests were either "slain in the spirit," or fell prostrate on their faces before God.

Take note, that it also mentions that Heman had three daughters who also participated in the Temple Worship. Women had more freedom under the Old Testament than what they do in some of the forms of Judaism today. I am confident that these three sisters were not the only women.

It is wonderful to know that women were included in the Temple Choir. God has given women beautiful voices. At times they sound like angels singing. Women did not only sing during the days of King David and King Solomon, we read that when the Children of Judah returned from captivity in Babylon the women still sang in the religious choir of their time, *"...And among them they had 200 men and women singers"* (Ezra 2:65). This is the choir that sang at the dedication of the Walls of Jerusalem when they were rebuilt.

Not only did they sing to worship the Lord, much of their music was prophetic music. They prophesied with instruments and with words. This means they had a very special anointing.

GOD LOVES A SINGER

The Lord God loves to hear us sing to Him our songs of love. Tagore expresses it so beautifully for us all:

"You came down from your throne, and stood at my cottage door. I was singing all alone in a corner, and the melody caught your ear. You came down and stood at my cottage door. Masters are many in your hall, and songs are sung there at all hours. But the simple carol of this novice struck at your love. One plaintive little strain, mingled with the great music of the world, and with a flower for a prize, you came down, and stopped at my cottage door."

Sometimes we hesitate to praise the Lord in song because we know we do not have beautiful voices, but even if we have but a "plaintive little strain" if it is filled with love, the Creator will leave the great orchestral music halls of Heaven, walk past the symphony orchestras and magnificent opera houses of today's finest singers, to stop at our humble cottage door, that He might only listen to our "plaintive little song."

When I was seventeen years old I had a beautiful voice. It was not trained, but I knew the gift I had was special. I dreamed of singing in the finest opera houses of this world. I spent many evenings, in my parent's home, singing classical music while my cousin, Hilda, accompanied me on the piano. One summer day, when the doors and windows of our house were open, because of the heat, there was a knock on the door. When I looked up, I saw a distinguished-looking, well-dressed man standing at the screen door. I welcomed him into the house, wondering who he was, and why he had come.

"I heard you singing, as I walked by, and I would so appreciate it, if I could just stay a while and listen," he said to me.

I was surprised, but I gladly welcomed him to stay, and I told him I would sing a song for him. I chose, "Among my Souvenirs," a song I loved. When I had finished singing, I saw him wipe away a tear.

"Surely, you could not have sung a more beautiful song for me," he said, softly.

I wondered what he meant by that. And then he introduced himself and told me his story. He was a famous Canadian, black singer of classical music who had given concerts all across Canada for many years. His wife, who had accompanied him on the piano, had just recently passed away. His heart was broken at the loss of his precious life's companion, and he had stopped singing.

"All I have left are souvenirs," he said to us. "Tomorrow, if I may, I will bring you my souvenirs, and show them to you."

And that he did. He brought a big box of newspaper clipping that he had cut out of papers in cities across the country, which described the concerts he had given. He had received many honours.

He told me that I needed to make singing my life's career. He took me to the Toronto Conservatory of

Music and introduced me to the president. I began studying voice. But shortly after that I was converted, and gave up my dreamed of career to follow the Lord's leading to go to Bible School, and prepare for the ministry. For years I sang for the nations, as I played my accordion. I believe that the Lord accomplished as much through my song as He ever did through any sermon I have ever preached.

Today I have lost my singing voice. But I still have a C.D. that was recorded in the days when God used my song to touch a hurting world.

The scribes of Israel say, "When a tune is played properly it has the power to beautify a person by uplifting his spirit, and to beautify the world around him." I long for the day when I can sing again.

STUDY QUESTIONS

1. Read 1 Chronicles chapters 15,16; 25:1-31, Acts 21-25.

2. Memorize Psalm 150, and name five of the instruments mentioned in it.

3. Who was the inventor of musical instruments? And why are instruments of music forbidden in some churches?

4. In what way are we musical instruments?

5. Why does God accept our song even though we are not talented to sing or play well?

CHAPTER ELEVEN

HEBREW WORDS FOR PRAISE

In the Old Testament there are many different Hebrew words for our one word, "Praise." It is important that we know a little about them so we can understand the in-depth meaning of what it really means to praise the Lord. Let us examine the following:

1288: *BARAK:* to bend the knee, to kneel down; to bless, praise, to be blessed, to praise; to pray to, to invoke, to ask a blessing. It was also considered a kindly or benevolent greeting from one person to another. This root and its derivative occur 415 times in the Old Testament (Judges 5:2).

1984: *HILLUWL:* (from 1984); a celebration of thanksgiving for harvest; merry, praise (Lev. 19:24).

1984: *HALAL:* to be bright, to shine; to be splendid; to boast; to praise, to celebrate, glorify; to be praised, to be famous; to cause to shine, to make bright, to give light; to deserve praise. At the heart of the Hebrew root is the idea of radiance. From this root came the connotation of the ebullience of rejoicing and praising God, the well-known imperative phrase in Hebrew, "hallelujah," called for giving the glory to God. There are instances where the word is applied to human beings (Gen. 12:15; 2 Sam. 14:25; 1 Kgs.20 11). We will hear this word many times in Heaven.

In 2 Chronicles 20:19 we read that when, in answer to their prayers and fasting, the prophets of the Lord prophesied that God would give Judah the victory against their enemies, the Levites *"stood up to praise (halal) the Lord God of Israel with a loud voice on high."*

In Psalm 34:2 it is translated "boast." *"My soul shall make her boast in the LORD: the humble shall hear thereof, and be glad"* (Psalms 34:2). When we praise the Lord, by boasting about Him to others, it gives joy to the humble who love the Lord.

2167: ZAMAR: This Hebrew verb means to harp or chord, to play, to make music, to sing, to sing praises, to celebrate. It is used almost exclusively in poetry, namely in songs. There are two passages which refer to songs in a negative sense (Isa 25:5; Amos 5:23).

3034: YADAH: To throw, to cast; to speak out, to confess; to praise, to sing, to give thanks, to thank. Essentially, it is the acknowledgment of sin, man's character, or the nature and work of God. The Hebrew syn. *halal* (1984) emphasizes pride in an object. *Yada* (3034) stresses recognition and declaration of a fact, whether it is good or bad. David made his sin known to God and did not attempt to hide it (Ps. 32:5). This verb is an expression of thanks to God by way of praising. In these contexts, "bless" would be a good translation. Praise leads to thanksgiving. The name, "Judah" comes from this root (Gen. 29:35).

7623: SHABACH: to address in a loud tone, to be loud; to glorify, to praise God for His mighty acts and deeds, (1 Chr. 16:35; Ps. 117:1; 145:4; 147:12); to boast (Ps. 106:47), to triumph; to pacify (through words), to calm anger (Prov. 29:11), to still, e.g. the waves, (Ps. 66:7; 89:9); to praise, i.e., soothe with praises (Ps. 63:3). The idea in Ps. 65:7 is to sooth, similar to the violent waves which Jesus calmed in Mat. 8:23-27. There are eleven occurrences in the Hebrew O.T.

8416: *TEHILLAH:* This feminine Hebrew noun is traceable to 1984. The meaning is laudation; a hymn (Ps. 22:4; 66:2; 145:1), praise (Ps. 22:26; 48:11; 51:17); a song of praise (a technical musical term for a song which exults God; (Ps. 145's title and Neh. 11:17), a psalm (the title to the entire Book of Psalms is in the plural form); a celebrity, glory, praiseworthiness (a quality describing God) (Deut. 10:21, Isa. 62:7); deeds which are worthy of praise (Ex. 15:11). This word occurs fifty-seven times in O.T.

8426: *TOWDAH:* this feminine Hebrew noun has its source in 3034. It means an extension of the hand, a confession (Josh. 7:19; Ezra 10:11); a vow; thanks, thanksgiving (Ps. 26:7; 42:5); a sacrifice of thanksgiving (Ps. 56:13); a type of peace offering (Lev. 7:12); offering praise to God for a sacrifice (Ps.50:14,23; 107:22, 116:17); a thanksgiving choir or procession who gave thanks in praising God (Neh.12:31; 8:4). This word appears about thirty times in the Hebrew O.T.

OTHER WORDS THAT EXPRESS PRAISE AND GRATITUDE

1523: *GUWL:* "to spin round (under the influence of any violent emotion) i.e. usually rejoicing; be glad, be joyful, rejoice" (Psalm 2:11, 21:1, 51:8, 53:6, 97:1, 118:24; Zechariah 4:10; Zephaniah 3:17)."

1921: *HADAR:* "to be large, swollen, to adorn, to decorate, to honour, to be esteemed, to be honoured, to boast, to act proudly. It has the idea of showing respect, especially to the elderly from the youth." It is translated in KJV as "goodly, glory, beauty, beauties, majesty, excellency, and comeliness" (Leviticus 23:40; Psalm 8:5; Proverbs 31:25; Isaiah 53:2).

7440: *RINNAH:* "cry, gladness, joy, proclamation, rejoicing, shouting, singing, triumph."

7812: *SHACHAH:* "to depress, to prostrate oneself (in homage or loyalty to God (Genesis 23:7, 37:7,9,10; Leviticus 26:1); to bow down (Isaiah 51:23); to crouch, to fall down, sink down, to humbly beseech, to do obeisance, to worship...In short, it was a way of showing submission (Psalm 45:11)."

8605: *TEPHILLAH* "this feminine noun is derived from 6419. It means intercession for someone, prayer, entreaty supplication, hymn. This is the most general Hebrew word of prayer in the Old Testament. Isaiah 56:7 states that God's house would be a house of prayer. Jesus quoted this verse when He "cleansed" the temple courtyard. *Tephillah* was used as a title in five Psalms, 17, 86, 90, 102, 142), and the title for the prayer of Habakkuk (3.1). The word appears in Psalm 72:20 to describe all the Psalms from Psalm 1 to Psalm 72, only one of which is truly a 'prayer' in the strict sense (Psalm 17:1). The term denotes a prayer which is set to music and sung in formal worship. It occurs seventy-seven times in the O.T."

8055 *SAMACH* "to brighten up, i.e. to make blithe or gleeful, to be glad, to make joyful, to make merry, to cause to rejoice (De.12:12; 1 Ch.16:10; Ps. 31:7, 58:10)."

As we study the different Hebrew words for praise we must realize that there are many ways in which we can, and should praise the Lord. We can see that the emotions can be very much involved; in fact the whole body can take part in praising the Lord. We can praise the Lord by twirling, dancing, jumping, rolling (like children, and youths who win a sports event sometimes do), by clapping, shouting, crying for joy, blowing the shofar, playing an instrument, etc. Let us therefore not limit our expressions of praise to God for all His greatness to a few, quiet words of thanksgiving. They are good, but we need to learn how to "explode" for the sheer joy of our "so great a salvation."

STUDY QUESTIONS

1. Read Acts chapters 26-28.

2. Research all of the above references.

3. Choose five Hebrew Words for "praise", and write a short truth on each one which could be used in a teaching.

CHAPTER TWELVE

EXCHANGE YOUR SPIRIT OF HEAVINESS FOR THE GARMENT OF PRAISE

Jesus did not only come to die for us and save us from eternal judgment, He came to give us joy and happiness.

While, it is a good thing to bring to God a "sacrifice of praise," our praises should not have to be a difficult thing to give God. We ought to be able to praise Him out of sheer joy, gratitude and thankfulness. It should be the expression of our heart.

God wants us to be a happy people. We are a better testimony to Him if we are happy than if we are mournful. Happy people don't have religious spirits.

Jesus, when reading from Isaiah at the synagogue in His home town of Nazareth said, *"The Spirit of the Lord GOD is upon me; because the LORD hath anointed me to preach good tidings unto the meek; he hath sent me to bind up the brokenhearted, to proclaim liberty to the captives, and the opening of the prison to them that are bound; To proclaim the acceptable year of the LORD, and the day of vengeance of our God; to comfort all that mourn; To appoint unto them that mourn in Zion, to give unto them beauty for ashes, the oil of joy for mourning, the garment of praise for the spirit of heaviness; that they might be called trees of righteousness, the planting of the LORD, that he might be glorified"* (Isaiah 61:1-3).

One might call this occasion the official introduction of the Messiah to His people. He was introduced as One who came to do good, to heal the brokenhearted, set the captives free, open prison doors. He had come as One who had an appointment with the mourners, the brokenhearted, whose lives lay in ashes at their feet, and who had long ago laid aside their festive robes of joy in exchange for the sackcloth of the mourner. He had come to break their chains of bondage, lift off their shoulders the heavy yoke of grief and slavery, and give them, instead, the joyous, beautiful garment of praise which the saints in Heaven wear.

This truth reveals to us the true heart of Our Father, His Son and the Holy Ghost who dwells within. The Glorious Trinity want us to live a life of joy that is filled with praises to God.

Psalm 30:11-12 says, *"Thou hast turned for me my mourning into dancing: thou hast put off my sackcloth, and girded me with gladness; To the end that my glory may sing praise to thee, and not be silent. O LORD my God, I will give thanks unto thee for ever."*

We do not have the strength to remove our sackcloth; it takes an act of God. The same One who has made for us garments of gladness, will miraculously disrobe us of our miserable spirit of heaviness, which is what the garment of sackcloth and mourning actually is.

I remember a period of my life when I was carrying such a spirit of heaviness that I could hardly minister without weeping. My heart was broken, and it had been broken for many years. Somehow, I just couldn't let go of that terrible pain that haunted me day and night.

And then one day, as I knelt to take Holy Communion in a Methodist Church in Karachi, Pakistan, I gave Him my broken heart. And He took it. I was instantly healed of deep, deep grief. It was instantaneous. It was glorious. I entered a new dimension of praise. That particular grief has never returned. It was a more miraculous healing to me than when I was healed of cancer and other afflictions. It was a healing of the soul.

The Lord wants to exchange your spirit of heaviness for a garment of Praise. He has a beautiful garment of praise, all glistening with fine gold, and studded with precious gems waiting for you in the Heavenly wardrobe. When you begin to praise Him, He will come down and clothe you in it.

The earth will be a beautiful place during the Millennium rule of Christ because it will be filled with praises. Psalm 69:34 says, *"Let the heaven and earth praise him, the seas, and every thing that moveth therein."*

Satan was the leader of praise in Heaven before he fell from his high and lofty position. His original name was Lucifer (Bright Morning Star). As the head praiser he allowed pride to enter his spirit. This led to rebellion against the Almighty. We may wonder how this can happen. It is because praise lifts us so high in the spirit that it brings us into a superlative realm of glory. When this happens we lose all consciousness of our limitations and we receive the imprint of the image of God. When this takes place it is possible to lose one's balance and reasoning. Soon one can think that they are "God Himself." In fact, this is the essence of New Age philosophy.

The New Agers get their "high" through hallucinating drugs, demons and deceptive doctrines of men. But, the sad thing is that Christians must also beware of the tricks and cunning devices of Satan. He can appear as an "angel of light," and before we realize it, we can receive that same spirit of deception. I have met Christians who thought they were little "gods."

Satan hates to hear us praising the Lord because it reminds him of the Glory he lost. Therefore he tries to hinder us from praising. But he will be bound and cast into the bottomless pit, so we will feel so pure and clean and free that we will be able to praise the Lord in the same way that the saints and angels praise Him in Heaven.

All of creation will join in praise to the Lord, even as is described in Psalm 148:1-13:

1 Praise ye the LORD. Praise ye the LORD from the heavens: praise him in the heights.

2 Praise ye him, all his angels: praise ye him, all his hosts.

3 Praise ye him, sun and moon: praise him, all ye stars of light.

4 Praise him, ye heavens of heavens, and ye waters that be above the heavens.

5 Let them praise the name of the LORD: for he commanded, and they were created.

6 He hath also stablished them for ever and ever: he hath made a decree which shall not pass.

7 Praise the LORD from the earth, ye dragons, and all deeps:

8 Fire, and hail; snow, and vapour; stormy wind fulfilling his word:

9 Mountains, and all hills; fruitful trees, and all cedars:

10 Beasts, and all cattle; creeping things, and flying fowl:

11 Kings of the earth, and all people; princes, and all judges of the earth:

12 Both young men, and maidens; old men, and children:

13 Let them praise the name of the LORD: for his name alone is excellent; his glory is above the earth and heaven"

A LITTLE CHINESE GIRL'S VISION

During a time of great revival in Macao the Holy Spirit gave Sen Ching, a precious ten-year-old Chinese girl, a wonderful vision of Heaven. I still have her lovely story, which I will share in part:

"I arrived at Heaven's gate. I was very happy. The place was as bright as the middle of the day. The first thing I saw, after coming inside, were the beautiful very high houses made of jewels and gold. I saw God's light. Heaven is brighter than the noon-day sun — many hundred times brighter. Jesus then came and changed my clothes to white.

"I wanted to find all my family, my grandma, and grandpa and aunties. I started looking all around. Some of them I could find, and some I could not see. Later my mother told me that those whom I could not find were not believers in the Lord Jesus. I was still looking for them when Jesus said, 'Praise the Lord!'

"Immediately, I began to praise Him with all my heart. Everyone around me was praising Him too. Some were dancing. They danced real high, clapping their hands. Everyone wore long shining clothes which reached down to the floor. Their faces were shining so brightly that I had to look and look at them.

"There were all kinds of instruments. Some that I had seen on earth, and some that I had never seen before. But they were made of jewels, and their sound was much more beautiful. I saw golden, shining pianos that were made with four keyboards in a square shape and four people played these pianos at a time. I saw four such pianos. The music was so beautiful that I cannot tell you how beautiful it really was. I had never heard anything so beautiful on earth. The faces of the people were the happiest I had ever seen. I also saw an accordion, and the straps of it were white and shining. The accordion was also made of jewels, and was white and shining.

"The angels flew around and around. There were many, many of them, and they praised the Lord all the time. All were dressed in white. The angels were truly happy. They wore a halo, and had big wings which reached down to their feet. Every angel held a golden trumpet, and when they played them, the music was so lovely that nothing can compare with it.

"The Lord Jesus' clothes were whiter than anyone else's — whiter than the angels' and whiter than the people's who had come to Heaven with me. A brownish-golden light shone all around Him. It seemed to shine from the jeweled crown which He was wearing. [She drew a picture of it for her mother]. His halo was bigger than the angels' halos were. His whole body shone, even his finger nails. His face and body was filled with grace. Jesus commanded, 'Praise!' and everyone praised. Greater joy fell on all. I was so happy, and I was praising Him so hard, when suddenly, my mother lifted me up, and all of Heaven's vision left me, and I was back on earth."

Sen Ching had given her heart to Jesus, and her entire vision also included the throne of judgment, but I only want to emphasize the joy of the saints and angels, and the praises that will radiate throughout Glory Land. Our Loved ones, who have gone on before us are up there praising the Lord right now and rejoicing in His wonderful Presence, while we are here on this sin-cursed earth, the habitat of demons. But we can have a little bit of Heaven if we will praise the Lord and sing and worship Him, for the demons cannot inhabit the praises of God's people, only God does.

If we tried to write all the truths about praise we would never be able to stop. This book would have no ending; but the purpose of this Bible-Study is not that we might gain more head-knowledge; rather it is meant to open our hearts to love and praise the Lord; for as we praise Him, He draws nigh to us, takes our hand, and leads us into His innermost Chambers of Love, where we fall on our knees in abandonment to His overwhelming love, and prostrate ourselves in worship at His throne together with the saints and twenty-four elders whom John saw, *"...fall down before him that sat on the throne, and worship him that liveth for ever and ever, and cast their crowns before the throne, saying, Thou art worthy, O Lord, to receive glory and honour and power: for thou hast created all things, and for thy pleasure they are and were created"* (Revelation 4:10-11).

I will meet you at the Throne-room!

Gwen R. Shaw
June 24, 2000

STUDY ASSIGNMENT

With the help of the Holy Spirit, sing in the Spirit Psalms 146 to Psalm 150. (You do not need to do them all at once. If you prefer, you can sing one every day for five days).

GWEN SHAW'S AUTOBIOGRAPHY!

UNCONDITIONAL SURRENDER—*Gwen Shaw.* The life story of Gwen R. Shaw, lovingly known as "Sister Gwen" to thousands of people in over one hundred nations. You will laugh and cry with her as you feel the heartbeat of a great woman of God who has given all to Him, asking only for souls in return. Your life will be challenged as you walk with her through mission field after mission field. You will never be the same when you read how God pours out His Spirit and confirms His Word.Hardcover #106-82 $19.95
..................................video NTSC (North American format) #GSL-99 $20.00
....................................video PAL (European format) #GSLP-99 $20.00

DAILY DEVOTIONALS BY GWEN SHAW

DAILY PREPARATIONS FOR PERFECTION —*Gwen Shaw.* This daily devotional comes to you exactly as the Holy Spirit spoke to the author's heart in her own private devotions. You will feel that Jesus is speaking to you every time you open it. It is loved by all; read and re-read ....Paperback #101-32 $12.50
DAY BY DAY—*Gwen Shaw.* The author's daily devotional book based on the Psalms will give you an inspiring word directly from the Throne Room each day to fill your heart with praise to God. It was a great comfort to the author herself after the fire in 1990 that destroyed so much. (Also available in French)..Hardcover #101-38 $18.50
FROM THE HEART OF JESUS—*Gwen Shaw.* This devotional book is like no other. It will take you back to Bible days and you will walk and talk with Jesus and His disciples as he ministered to the people, as He suffered and died and as He rose again from the dead. These words from the heart of Jesus will go straight to your heart, bringing comfort, peace encouragement and hope! 923 pages ....Hardcover #102-11 $29.95
GEMS OF WISDOM — A daily devotional based on the book of Proverbs — *Gwen Shaw.* In the Proverbs you will find instruction for upright living, honesty, justice and wisdom. Every word in the Proverbs applies to today's problems as when they were first written. If you are going through great difficulties and facing problems which seem to have no solution, you will find the answer in these Proverbs. You'll have a Proverb and an inspired writing about it for each day of the year ....Hardcover #105-49 $25.95
IN THE BEGINNING — A daily devotional based on the book of Genesis — *Gwen Shaw.* The Book of Genesis is perhaps the most important Book in the Old Testament. It is the foundation stone of all knowledge and wisdom. Deep and wonderful truths hidden in the pages of Genesis are revealed in this devotional book. You'll be amazed at the soul-stirring writings inspired by the well-known stories of Genesis ....#115-47 $27.95

Ad 1

CLASSIC ANOINTED BIBLE STUDIES

BEHOLD THE BRIDEGROOM COMETH!— *Gwen Shaw.* A Bible study on the soon return of Jesus Christ. With so many false teachings these days, it is important that we realize how imminent the rapture of the saints of God really is ....#100-37 $6.50

ENDUED WITH LIGHT TO REIGN FOREVER — *Gwen Shaw.* This deeply profound Bible study reveals the characteristics of the eternal, supernatural, creative light of God as found in His Word. The "Father of Lights," created man in His image. He longs for man to step out of darkness and into His light ....#101-71 $6.00

GOD'S END-TIME BATTLE-PLAN—*Gwen Shaw.* This study on spiritual warfare gives you the biblical weapons for spiritual warfare such as victory through dancing, shouting, praising, uplifted hands, marching, etc. It has been a great help to many who have been bound by tradition ....#102-35 $8.00

IT'S TIME FOR REVIVAL—*Gwen Shaw.* A Bible Study on Revival that not only gives scriptural promises of the end-time Revival, but also presents the stories of revivals in the past and the revivalists whom God used. It will stir your heart and encourage you to believe for great revival ......#103-24 $7.75

OUR MINISTERING ANGELS—*Gwen Shaw.* A scriptural Bible study on the topic of angels. Angels will be playing a more and more prominent part in these last days. We need to understand about them and their ministry ....#104-87 $7.50

POUR OUT YOUR HEART—*Gwen Shaw.* A wonderful Bible study on travailing prayer. The hour has come to intercede before the throne of God. The call to intercession is for everyone, and we must carry the Lord's burden and weep for the lost so that the harvest can be brought in quickly ....#105-16 $5.00

REDEEMING THE LAND—*Gwen Shaw.* This important teaching will help you know your authority through the Blood of Jesus to dislodge evil spirits, break the curse, and restore God's blessing upon the land. A Bible study on spiritual warfare..#108-61 $9.50

THE FINE LINE—*Gwen Shaw.* This Bible study clearly magnifies the "fine line" difference between the soul realm and the spirit realm. Both are intangible and therefore cannot be discerned with the five senses, but must be discerned by the Holy Spirit and the Word of God. A must for the deeper Christian..#101-91 $6.00

THE POWER OF THE PRECIOUS BLOOD—*Gwen Shaw.* A Bible study on the Blood of Jesus. The author shares how it was revealed to her how much Satan fears Jesus' Blood. This Bible study will help you overcome and destroy the works of Satan in your life and the lives of loved ones ....#105-18 $5.00

THE POWER OF PRAISE—*Gwen Shaw.* When God created the heavens and earth He was surrounded by praise. Miracles happen when holy people praise a Holy God! Praise is the language of creation. If prayer can move the hand of God, how much more praise can move Him! ....#400-66 $5.00

YE SHALL RECEIVE POWER FROM ON HIGH *Gwen Shaw.* This is a much needed foundational teaching on the Baptism of the Holy Spirit. It will enable you to teach this subject, as well as to understand these truths more fully yourself...#107-37 $5.00

YOUR APPOINTMENT WITH GOD—*Gwen Shaw.* A Bible study on fasting. Fasting is one of the most neglected sources of power over bondages of Satan that God has given the Church. The author's experiences are shared in this Bible study in a way that will change your life ....#107-40 $5.00

IN-DEPTH BIBLE STUDIES

FORGIVE AND RECEIVE—An In-Depth Bible Study on Philemon for the Serious Student of God's Word—*Gwen Shaw.* This Bible Study is a lesson to the church on the much-needed truths of forgiveness and restoration. The epistle to Philemon came from the heart of Paul who had experienced great forgiveness ....#102-01 $7.00

GRACE ALONE—An In-Depth Bible Study on Galatians for the Serious Student of God's Word—*Gwen Shaw.* This study teaches the reader to gain freedom in the finished work of the Cross by forsaking works which cannot add to salvation and live by *Grace Alone* ....#108-47 $13.00

MYSTERY REVEALED—An In-Depth Bible Study on Ephesians for the Serious Student of God's Word—*Gwen Shaw.* Search the depths of God's riches in one of Paul's most profound epistles, "to the praise of His glory!" Learn the "mystery" of the united Body of Christ........#104-53 $15.00

OUR GLORIOUS HEAD—An In-Depth Bible Study on Colossians for the Serious Student of God's Word—*Gwen Shaw.* This book teaches vital truths for today, assisting the reader in discerning false teachings, when the philosophies of men are being promoted as being the truths of God. Jesus Christ is the Head of His Body ....#104-85 $9.00

THE CATCHING AWAY!—An In-Depth Bible Study on First and Second Thessalonians —*Gwen Shaw.* This is a very timely Bible Study because Jesus is coming soon! The book of I Thessalonians explains God's revelation to Paul on the rapture of the saints. II Thessalonians reveals what will happen after the rapture when the antichrist takes over ....#100-88 $13.00

THE LOVE LETTER—An In-Depth Bible Study on Philippians for the Serious Student of God's Word—*Gwen Shaw.* Another of Gwen Shaw's expository Bibles Studies on the books of the Bible. This study of the letter to the first church of Europe will give the reader an understanding of Paul's great love for the church that was born out of his suffering ....#103-99 $9.00

BIBLE COURSE

THE TRIBES OF ISRAEL—*Gwen Shaw.* This popular and well-loved study on the thirteen tribes of Israel will show you your place in the spiritual tribes in these last days. Better understand yourself and others through the study of this Bible Course ....#106-70 $45.00

OTHER BOOKS BY GWEN SHAW

LOVE, THE LAW OF THE ANGELS—*Gwen Shaw.* This is undoubtedly the greatest of Gwen Shaw's writings. It carries a message of healing and life in a sad and fallen civilization. Love heals the broken-hearted and sets disarray in order. You will never be the same after reading this beautiful book about love. (Also available in French) ....Paperback #103-97 $10.00

SONG OF LOVE—*Gwen Shaw.* She was a heart-broken missionary, far from home. She cried out to God for help. He spoke, "Turn to the Song of Solomon and read!" As she turned in obedience, the Lord took her into the "Throne Room" of Heaven and taught her about the love of Christ for His Bride, the church. She fell in love with Jesus afresh, and you will too ....#108-62 $7.50

THE FALSE FAST — *Gwen Shaw.* Now, from the pen of Gwen Shaw, author of *Your Appointment With God* (a Bible Study on fasting), comes an exposé on the False Fast. It will help you to examine your motives for fasting, and make your foundations sure, so that your fast will be a potent tool in the hands of God 115-62 $2.50

THE LIGHT WILL COME FROM RUSSIA — *Gwen Shaw.* The thrilling testimony of Mother Barbara, Abbess of the Mount of Olives in Jerusalem. She shares prophecies which were given to her concerning the nations of the world in our time by a holy bishop of the Kremlin, ten days before his death just prior to the Russian Revolution ....#116-24 $3.95

TO BE LIKE JESUS — *Gwen Shaw.* Based on her Throne Room experience in 1971, the author shares the Father's heart about our place as sons in His Family. Nothing is more important than *To Be Like Jesus!* ....#116-51 $6.95

THE PARABLE OF THE GOLDEN RAIN—*Gwen Shaw.* This is the story of how revivals come and go, and a true picture, in parable language, of how the Church tries to replace the genuine move of the Spirit with man-made programs and tactics. It's amusing and convicting at the same time ....#104-94 $4.00

THEY SHALL MOUNT UP WITH WINGS AS EAGLES—*Gwen Shaw.* Though you may feel old or tired, if you wait on the Lord, you shall mount up on wings as eagles! Let this book encourage you to stretch your wings and fulfill your destiny—no matter what your age! ....#116-22 $6.95

POCKET SERMON BOOKS BY GWEN SHAW

BEHOLD, THIS DREAMER COMETH — *Gwen Shaw.* Dreams and dreamers are God's gift to humanity to bring His purposes into the hearts of mankind. This message of the life of Joseph, the dreamer, will encourage you to believe God to fulfill the dream He has put into your heart................#118-30 $1.50

BREAKTHROUGH — *Gwen Shaw.* If you need a "breakthrough" in your life, this book reveals the truth in a fresh and living way! ....#200-47 $1.50

DON'T STRIKE THE ROCK! — *Gwen Shaw.* Moses first struck the Rock in obedience. When he became bitter and angry with the rebellion of the people and disobeyed God's new order to speak to the Rock, it cost him his entrance into the Promised Land. Don't allow anything to keep you from fulfilling God's perfect will for your life! ....#114-43 $1.50

HASTENING OUR REDEMPTION — *Gwen Shaw.* All of Heaven and Earth are waiting for the Body of Christ to rise up in maturity and reclaim what we lost in the Fall of Man. Applying the Blood of Jesus is the key to ***Hastening Our Redemption*** ....#116-53 $1.50

IT CAN BE AVERTED — *Gwen Shaw.* Many people today are burdened and fearful over prophecies of doom and destruction. However, the Bible is clear that God prefers mercy over judgment when His people humble themselves and pray ....#116-85 $1.50

KAIROS TIME — *Gwen Shaw.* That once in a lifetime opportunity—that second, or minute, or hour, or year, or even longer, when a golden opportunity is sovereignly given to us by the Almighty. What we do with it can change our lives and possibly even change the world ....#200-06 $1.50

KNOWING ONE ANOTHER IN THE SPIRIT—*Gwen Shaw.* Experience great peace as you learn to understand the difficulties your friends, enemies and loved ones face that help to form their character. *"Wherefore henceforth know we no man after the flesh.."* (II Corinthians 5:16a). An anointed message in booklet form ....#103-62 $1.50

THE CRUCIFIED LIFE—*Gwen Shaw.* When you suffer and you know the cause is not your own sin, for you have searched your heart before God; then you must accept that it is God doing a new thing in yoru life. Let joy rise up within you because you are a partaker of Christ's suffering ....#115-61 $1.50

THE MASTER IS COME AND CALLETH FOR THEE — *Gwen Shaw.* Read about how the Lord called Gwen Shaw to begin the ministry of the End-Time Handmaidens and Servants. Perhaps the Master is also calling you into His service. Bring Him the fragments of your life — He will put them together again. An anointed message booklet ....#104-31 $1.50

WOMEN OF THE BIBLE SERIES

EVE—MOTHER OF US ALL — *Gwen Shaw.* Discover the secrets of one of the most neglected and misunderstood stories in history ....#117-50 $4.50

MIRIAM—THE PROPHETESS — *Gwen Shaw.* The first female to lead worship, the first woman given the title "Leader" of God's people by the Lord ....#M400-67 $7.50

SARAH—PRINCESS OF ALL MANKIND — *Gwen Shaw.* Feel the heartbeat and struggles of this woman who left so great an impact for all time ....#117-51 $4.50

REBEKAH—THE BRIDE — *Gwen Shaw.* The destiny of the world was determined when she says three simple words, "I will go!" ......#117-52 $4.50

LEAH AND RACHEL—THE TWIN WIVES OF JACOB — *Gwen Shaw.* You will feel their dreams, their pains, their jealousies ....#200-46 $4.50

BOOKS PUBLISHED BY ENGELTAL PRESS

ATTITUDES IN THE BEATITUDES — *Esther Rollins.* Esther taught this anointed course on the Beatitudes as a guest teacher at our School of Ministry and an instructor of the Word of God for 50 years. Both basic and profound, this dynamic teaching is full of insight for the Christian walk ....#115-72 $5.95
BANISHED FOR FAITH — *Emil Waltner.* The stirring story of the courageous forefathers of Gwen Shaw, the Hutterite Mennonites, who were banished from their homeland and suffered great persecution for their faith. Republished with an index and epilogue by Gwen Shaw ....#100-33 $12.95
BECOMING A SERVANT — *Robert Baldwin.* Learn what is on God's heart about servanthood. We must learn to serve before we can be trusted to lead. If you want to be great in God's Kingdom, learn to be the servant of all ....#118-55 $2.00
FOOTPRINTS — *Larry Hunt.* A collection of poems and stories reflecting the hand of God upon this humble pastor during 35 years of ministry ....#114-25 $3.75
FROM DUST TO GLORY — *June Lewis.* The Lord intends more than just salvation for us. He is making vessels of eternal Glory if we submit to Him. A collection of poems and stories reflecting the hand of God upon this humble pastor during 35 years of ministry ....#102-07 $7.50
HOLY ANN — *Helen Bingham.* This humble Irish woman moved the arm of God through simple faith and prevailing prayer. Read these modern miracles that are told like a story from the Old Testament. The record of a lifetime of answered prayer ....#110-38 $4.95
IT WAS WORTH IT ALL — *Elly Matz.* The story of a beautiful woman whose courage will inspire you. Feel HER heart as she tells of her starving father, the young Communist engineer she married, the villages mysteriously evacuated, the invading German army, the concentration camp where she was a prisoner, and her escape into freedom ....#115-70 $5.95
LET'S KEEP MOVING — *Pete Snyder.* Travel with Peter to Haiti where he struggles with the call of God to be a missionary. Identify with Peter's growth of faith through trials and tribulations as he travels on to China where new adventures await and a kind endurance is needed ....#115-71 $9.95
RULING IN THEIR MIDST — *June Lewis.* The Lord has called us to rule even in the midst of all demonic activity and Satan's plans and schemes. Sister June has learned spiritual warfare from the Lord Himself, "who teacheth my hands to war," in the face of personal tragedy ....#108-73 $6.00
THE EYE OF THE NEEDLE — *Charlotte Baker.* These heavily anointed, life-changing prophetic parables will be used of the Holy Spirit to touch the depths of you and minister to your greatest needs ....#113-22 $3.00

THE GOLDEN AGE OF RETIREMENT — *Gen Siewiorek.* With humor and spiritual insight the author welcomes you to the world of retirement homes. She examines such sensitive and painful issues as losing one's independence, adjusting to the food and activities of retirement home living and facing what it means to grow old and eventually die ......#G400-68 $10.95

THE STORY OF THE GLORY — *Robert Doorn.* The Glory of God has followed Drs. Robert and Glenyce Doorn throughout their fifty years of ministry. You will be blessed as you witness almost every great move of God through their eye ....#118-77 $9.95

WESLEY'S SERMONS — *John Wesley.* Five sermons by this great saint whose love and compassion for souls helped produce the Great Awakening ....#107-00 $4.50

BOOKS RECOMMENDED BY ENGELTAL PRESS

AWAKENED BY AN ANGEL — *Carl W. Hahn, Jr.* Read the daily and nightly accounts of a retired denominational pastor who has been seeing light forms of angels and recording his experiences ever since ....#A400-26 $12.00

EDITED BY AN ANGEL — *Carl W. Hahn, Jr.* The continuing saga of Rev. Hahn's experiences as his Guardian Angel Precious assists in editing his book from his daily and nightly visitations ....#E400-030 $12.00

EVIDENCES OF THE FOOTPRINTS OF GOD— *Tommy Schmidt.* You will be thrilled with some of the wonderful facts and truths of the science of creation and the mysteries of the creative works of God ....#E118-69 $15.00

OH THAT ISHMAEL MIGHT LIVE — *Gene Little.* Through the author's love for the Muslim people which grew out of his journeys to the nations of this world, learn to overcome your fears and ignorance and bring life to Abraham's forgotten sons and daughters ....#O116-56 $15.00

TO LOVE A STRANGER — *Gene Little.* A biblical study introducing you to the blessings of hospitality and honors given to a Christian through the ministry of an open heart and open door ....#T113-11 $5.00

WELLSPRING OF WISDOM — *Gene Little.* The stories Jesus told centuries ago are as fresh today as they were two thousand years ago. Each generation has tried to catch these truths and insights. Be renewed in your faith and refreshed in the Spirit of Jesus through His parables ....#W300-38 $15.00

BOOKS ABOUT HEAVEN

INTRA MUROS — *Rebecca Springer.* One of the most beautiful books about Heaven available in its unabridged form. Read the glorious account of this ordinary believer's visit to Heaven ....#103-19 $8.00

PARADISE, THE HOLY CITY AND TH GLORY OF THE THRONE — *Elwood Scott.* Visited by a saint of God who spent forty days in Heaven, Elwood Scott's detailed description will edify and comfort your heart. Especially good for those with lost loved ones ....#104-97 $8.00

CHILDREN'S BOOKS

LITTLE ONES TO HIM BELONG—*Gwen Shaw.* Based on the testimonies of children's visions of Heaven and the death of a small Chinese boy, Sister Gwen weaves a delightful story of the precious joys of Heaven for children of all ages ....#103-88 $9.00

TELL ME THE STORIES OF JESUS—*Gwen Shaw.* Sister Gwen takes some of the greatest New Testament Stories of the Life of Jesus and writes them in a way that will interest children and help them to love Jesus........#106-37 $9.00

PROPHECIES AND VISIONS

THE DAY OF THE LORD IS NEAR: Vol. I - IV—*Engeltal Press.* "Surely the Lord GOD will do nothing, but he revealeth his secret unto his servants the prophets." (Amos 3: 7) A collection of prophecies, visions and dreams. This startling compilation will help you understand what God has in His heart for the near future ....$10.00 each
....Volumes I - IV with binder-10#119-99 $25.00

Prices are subject to change without notice.
You may obtain a current price list from

Engeltal Press
P.O. Box 447 • Jasper, Ark. 72641
Phone (870) 446-2665 • Fax (870) 446-2259
www.engeltalpress.com